Lola

Sadie

think pink

I'd like to send glitter-filled wishes and lip-gloss kisses to:

My biggest crush and leading man, Anthony – for dealing with my foot-stompin' tantrums
and for being really rather fabulous (not to mention cute to look at) on a daily basis – love you!

My very own pink ladies – ed girl Lindsey Kelk, agent lady Julia Churchill
and chief cheerleader/mentor Cathy Cassidy - for being super-talented, super-supportive
and for Thinking Pink from the get-go, I'm a lucky lady to have such an all-star girl gang!

The parentals – popashongo, mum and John – for your endless support and love.
Susie, Sarah B, Sarah C, Vicky, Stephen B, Mark W, Brett, DK
and all my amazing be-there-buds for never, ever doubting me.

Techno boy Jason Nelson – for spending the past four years
immersed in all things pink and fluffy – you rule.

And to all the feisty, fun, fearless and fabulous Pink Ladies who have
visited the website and made pink-world their home, this is for you –
the pink revolution starts here girls!

First published in Great Britain by HarperCollins Children's Books in 2007
HarperCollins Children's Books is a division of HarperCollinsPublishers Ltd,
77 – 85 Fulham Palace Road, Hammersmith, London, W6 8JB
The HarperCollins children's website address is www.harpercollinschildrensbooks.co.uk
The Pink World Website is at www.pink-world.co.uk
1 3 5 7 9 10 8 6 4 2
ISBN-13: 978-0-00-723401-1
ISBN-10: 0-00-723401-5
Printed and bound in China
Text © 2007 Lisa Clark
Illustrations by Holly Lloyd @ Lemonade © HarperCollins Childrens' Books

think pink

By **Lisa Clark**

HarperCollins *Children's Books*

Introduction

If you're fed up with your current dull and dreary existence, put on a pair of pink tinted shades and see the world through the eyes of the feisty, fun, fearless and fabulous... **Lola Love**.

That's me, by the way! I will offer you exclusive access to the most exciting, full-to-the-brim world of opportunities and possibilities, a place where kooky chicks rule and boys are all beautiful and without complication... Mmm, let's pause on that thought for a moment.

A place where you can crown yourself princess and wear your tiara with your pyjamas and most importantly, a place where you can shine because, let's face it, you are a star!

It's all about me...

Name... Lola Love

Age... 14

Hair colour (at the moment)... Pink – well, you'd expect nothing less, would you?

I ❤... Movies – they're the perfect escape route for when real life gets... well, too real lifey... Vintage dresses... Amelie – she's a raven haired, magic girl - I love her... Hair flickin' and air kissin' with my very own Pink Ladies, my best friends in the entire world – Angel, Bella and Sadie... Old movie stars from the fifties like Audrey Hepburn, Marilyn Monroe and Jane Mansfield, oh my stars, they were by far the most glamorous women your eyes will ever have seen... 60's soul music – perfect for shaking your booty...Ice cream-flavoured, sunny Sundays spent in the park... Sparkly tiaras... Laughing out loud... Shoes – they're my weakness!... Chickflick watching – take any of the following: Clueless, Pretty in Pink, Grease, or Mean Girls, add a generous helping of cookie dough ice cream, your own Pink Ladies and voila, you've got yourself the perfect sleepover combination... My ceramic hair straighteners – the ultimate in kink-busting... Glitterballs - making every night a disco in my bedroom... Taking photos - everyone should have a photo-girl phase... Customising clothes... Sleeping – actually, that should have been at the top of the list. I'm officially the self-crowned queen of sleeping, I like it a lot... Sand between my toes and shaggy-haired, guitar-playing indie rock boys – if loving them is wrong then I don't want to be right...

Hey chicas, welcome to my world!

I'm here to rescue the dull and the dreary amongst you from the miserable and unfortunate place that I used to cohabit on a daily basis...the real world.

Instead, I want to introduce you to a world that is best viewed through a pair of pink-tinted shades...Pink World!

In Pink World, you can banish miserably monotone thoughts of chubby tummies, bad school marks and argumentative parentals and replace them with the most exciting possibilities – to dream hugely, be inspired and wear whatever you want without fear of ridicule. You can be a 'Go-For-It' girl with a lust for life who refuses to take 'no' for an answer and, most importantly, indulge yourself on a regular basis because, quite frankly, you're worth it.

Now, a visit to Pink World is guaranteed to make you feel fabulous but if you would like to become the feisty, fun, fearless and fabulous star-shine girl you are destined to be, then you've got to live your life permanently in the pink...You've got to Think Pink so read on...

The Think Pink manifesto

Don't wait for others to treat you like the princess that you are. Have a full-to-the-brim bubble bath at two o'clock in the afternoon, be creative, eat copious amounts of chocolate, read a whole book in one sitting, watch your favourite film for the 84th time, take regular naps, add your own here...

Write lists
Not only do they stop you forgetting the important things, they help to create purpose and set goals, oh, and they also remind you where you saw that to-die-for pair of sequin-spangled killer boots!

Be a 'Go-For-It' girl
Develop a 'can-do' mentality by trying food you've never tasted without turning your nose up. If there's something you're scared of doing then face that fear, think positively and believe that you can do anything – go get 'em girl!

Reinvent yourself when necessary
If you're unhappy with something, change it! Don't be afraid to try new things, whether it's pink fishnet tights, a new haircut or thinking differently about something or someone.

Tell the boy-types to get in line
Don't get me wrong, they make good arm candy but they can't beat a night in with your giggle girls or a bowl of Angel Delight or my gorgeous new pink hat, scarf and mittens combo.

Be a trailblazer
Whether it's wearing flip-flops in the rain, wanting to be the first girl on Mars or choosing what course to take, don't follow in the footstep of others, go where there is no path and make your own high-heeled-shaped footprints.

Dare to dream
Dream hugely, don't put limitations on yourself because in Pink World anything is possible. I change my mind about what I want to be at least once a week, just because I can!

Search for a hero
We all need someone to show us how great the world can be, someone who has lived a

little and is willing to share their story, someone who is able to give us a butt-kick in the right direction. I've got a journal full of amazing ladies who rock my world; celebrities, friends, artists, entrepreneurs, family members but ultimately, YOU should be the shiniest heroine-shaped star in your world.

Always smile
It goes with everything - it's the perfect accessory!

Celebrate being a girl
If you're a girl that means you're not a boy and that's got to be a good thing! For us, pink is a do-able colour, we can turn an outfit from 'bland' to 'grand' just by adding accessories, we have kick-ass sleepovers with chocolate and chickflicks, we can talk on the phone for hours about nothing and most importantly, we get a much bigger selection of shoes!

When you Think Pink, anything is possible, you can live a life filled with thousands of candy kissed, sunshine moments because you're the one in control.

What could be more exciting than that?

I guarantee that once you've seen the world through my pink-tinted shades you'll never want to take them off!

If you're unhappy with something, change it!

big up yourself

'CHICA, YOU RULE!'

'*It's official, I rock!*'

Whether it's making friends, passing exams, getting an allowance increase or bagging a buff boy – being a feisty, fun, fearless and fabulous princess of pink world is a sure-fire way of getting what you want out of life and, once you've discovered the fantastic things that can happen when you Think Pink, it will quite possibly be the most exciting, sunshine-splashed experience...ever!

Before seeing the world through pink-tinted shades there were some days when I just didn't feel like the star-shaped sparkle girl that I actually am. I'd look in the mirror and become queen of the putdowns, I just couldn't see past the spot on my chin or the size of my bum. This would be an instant excuse for me to hide under the duvet indefinitely with a family size pack of biscuits wallowing in bad thoughts and self-doubt.

....Think Pink, it will quite possibly be the most exciting, sunshine-splashed experience...ever!

What you see when you look in the mirror depends on whether you're a self-esteem queen or an esteem-lacking Lucy. Self-esteem is an essential item in the Think Pink vanity case. If you have it, you like yourself, you're confident and you're satisfied with being you.

Unfortunately, loving and accepting yourself is not something you can buy in a tub at the cosmetics counter (oh my stars, how fabulous would that be?) and for some it takes much longer to discover than others, but Think Pink and you will be well on your way to becoming your very own dream girl.

Are you a self-esteem queen?

Are you happy being you or are you in need of a bravado boost?

When you walk past a mirror, do you:
a. turn and run in the opposite direction
b. take a good look and smile at what you see

Do you believe you can do whatever you want to in life?
a. it's nice to dream but they never come true, so no
b. with a lot of hard work you can do anything, so yes

You're meeting your Pink Ladies for a slice of chocolate cake, but when you arrive they go quiet, do you:
a. feel awkward. They could have been talking about you
b. ask them what the latest gossip is!

When the cute boy behind the counter winks at you, do you:
a. look behind you to see who he's winking at
b. smile your sweetest smile back at him

When you think about how you look, do you:
a. feel uncomfortable and wrong
b. feel happy and content

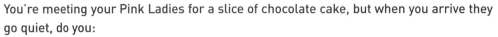

Mostly a's
You're an amazing person but sometimes you need a reminder of just how cool you are. A quick way to boost your bravado is to try little confidence tricks like smiling at people and keeping eye contact. Try to set yourself some cool challenges like getting involved in a new activity, your confidence will grow and you'll have a great time too!

Mostly b's...
You're a self-esteem queen! You seem to be blush-free, in control and sorted, you lucky lady. You don't let anything hold you back and are positively filled-to-the-brim with self-belief – keep it up, chica!

Don't believe the hype

I used to have the hugest hang up about my weight. This was due to an over-zealous stick-thin cousin who thought it would be mucho fun to laugh at my chubby tummy at every available opportunity. I remember feeling my curvaceous contours and despising them. They made me want to look like her, instead of being happy with being me. I'd feel so inadequate and unnecessary that I'd think nothing of eating five doughnuts in a row and telling myself how grimsville I was.

Most of us put ourselves down because of the unhelpful messages that have been fired in our direction by the 'Negative Ninas' of the world – teachers giving us a low mark, our so-called mate not picking us for the hockey team, parents saying we've done something wrong – the list is endless.

These nasty-rude comments and actions can knock our confidence faster than a ten-pin bowler, the trick is to not let this happen. Living the rest of your life according to what other people think of you is going to be a serious waste of your time and energy and will stop you from doing all the amazingly fantastic things you are destined to do. Let any negative vibes bounce off your sparkly-gorgeous tiara and, instead, lose yourself in thoughts of how fantastically fabulous you are because when you ignore others' mistreatment of your gorgeous self, the world will become a decidedly deeper shade of pink!

Most of us put ourselves down because of the unhelpful messages that have been fired in our direction by the 'Negative Ninas' of the world.

aka 'Negative Ninas'

Boost your bravado!

Think about how great you feel when you put on your all time favourite outfit with those to-die-for pair of atomic-pink kitten heeled mules. You feel like you can take on the world, right? That's because you've wrapped yourself up in a prize-winning package that makes you feel sparkly-gorgeous fantastic. Now imagine feeling like that every day...well, you can! You see, when you feel that great about yourself, you automatically stand taller, smile more and ooze confidence – this instantly makes you decidedly more attractive and a whole lot of fun to be around. Boost your bravado on a regular basis by:

✫ **Making a statement**
Start by looking in the mirror. Smile, grab your hairbrush and get that all-important dose of self-esteem pumping by belting out Christina's 'Beautiful' loud enough to shatter glass. Alternatively, choose a positive statement that will have the same feel-good factor and write it down. Stick a copy on your mirror, in your school book, make it a screensaver on your computer, anywhere that you look on a regular basis, as this will become a constant reminder of how cool you really are!

✫ **Be good to yourself**
Don't beat yourself up because you don't look like someone in the pages of a magazine (I'll let you into an industry secret - they're all airbrushed by techno peeps on computers anyway!) Instead, love the things that make you the feisty, fun, fearless and fabulous YOU.

✫ **Celebrate you**
Here in Pink World anything from passing an exam to tidying your room deserves celebrating, so reward yourself with a treat of your choice. Naturally, mine would be chocolate!

...Don't beat yourself up because you don't look like someone in the pages of a magazine...

Lose your label

I surprised everyone, not to mention myself, when I unleashed the real me onto the world. People had always thought of Lola Love as the 'weird writing girl.' They had given me a label that looked set to stick. Now don't get me wrong, I was a little bit weird in a cool and kooky way and I did, and still do, love to write. But there was a whole lot more to me than just those things and I wanted the world to know about them. Except, I was too scared.

Y'see, the popular girls wore their 'too-cool-for-school' badges with pride and the fit, football playing dudes of the playground were more than happy to live up to their 'sports jock' title. Nobody really questioned their labels, even the people with bad ones like 'shallow diva' or 'flirty floozy' so how was I ever going to lose mine?

By being who I was destined to be without worrying about what people thought, that's how. I know it's easier said than done, but by ditching the pressure of what other people thought of me, I became free to be the sparkle-shine girl I'd always wanted to be, not who other people expected me to be.

There are some labels I'm sure you'd be more than happy to carry around, Prada being one of mine, but if you're not digging the badge you've been given, hand it back and make your own!

What label would you like to ditch?

....

....

....

....

....

What would you like people to know about you?

....

....

....

....

....

....

Shameless self-promotion

As any successful, kick-ass chick will tell you, if you want to get ahead in life, you'll need to be super confident, know what you're good at and maximise your potential. So, forget big name brands like Nike and Coca-Cola, make 'brand YOU' the most successful, exciting and fantastically fabulous brand on the market. Check me out!

Brand: Lola Love – Pink Princess
Main features: Feisty, fun, fearless and fabulous
Unique Selling Point: My pink hair!
Packaging: In-your-face, original and creative
Content: Funny, unique, kooky, determined and genuine
Tag line: I Rock!

In order to tell the world how sparkly-gorgeous you are, you need to sell yourself baby!

Brand: who are you and what do you want to be seen as?

....
....
....
....
....
....
....
....
....

Main features: what makes you so amazing?

....
....
....
....
....
....
....
....
....

Unique Selling Point: What makes you stand out from everyone else?

....

....

....

....

....

....

....

....

Packaging: How would you describe yourself?

....

....

....

....

....

....

....

....

Content: What are your kick-ass qualities?

....

....

....

....

....

....

....

Tag line: How would you sum yourself up in one sentence?

....

....

....

....

Now read it and believe it, start believing the hype, because when you believe in yourself and all the things that make you great, you will rule the world!

Motivating Mantras

For those moments when you don't feel like the sparkle-shine glitter girl that you really are, mutter a marvellous mantra. A mantra is a few simple words, a phrase or a sentence that will boost your motivation and confidence and encourage you to Think Pink. I've got them everywhere, on my mirror, in my school books and I've even sewn 'you rock' onto my school bag – I'm so art girl! These are a few of my favourites, cut them out, tape them up and be inspired!

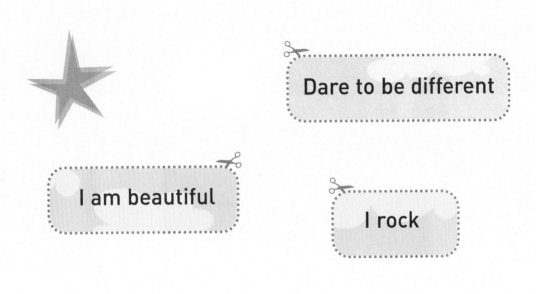

Dare to be different

I am beautiful

I rock

Happiness isn't having what you want – it's wanting what you have

Fake it 'til you make it

Last year, when the poster went up for the school production of Grease, I wanted nothing more than to play the part of Frenchy – she's a fun and fabulous, pink-haired kinda girl who rocks my world. Angel, my best friend and real-life Frenchy (you'll meet her later, she's super sassy and allsorts of fabulous) was relentless and would not rest her shiny-glossed lips until I agreed to audition. Thing is, I was scared, super scared. I thought I would make a prize plum of myself and I doubted my abilities. So I faked it.

I pretended I was Marilyn Monroe, all graceful and beautiful and adored by millions, auditioning for the role. You see, Marilyn was far too cool and talented not to get the part. So as I stepped up to the stage, I instantly became tall, proud and confident. Thankfully, acting like you're confident tends to make you feel confident and once I had belted out 'Beauty School Dropout' I knew I was rockin'! It worked, I bagged the role, the play was hugely successful and I was so confident in my own acting abilities that I left Marilyn at home throughout the whole production.

This technique can be applied to any situation. If you've got a date with that oh-so-fine, hot-to-trot chico then pretend to be a celeb type who everyone admires for their sparkling wit and melt-heart eyes. If you're nervous about a sports match, pick your favourite athlete and pretend to be her. Faking confidence is a great way to prove you can do it, get through it, realise you rock and have the real confidence to go solo next time!

Lola's top five confidence tricks...

1. Walk tall. I know it sounds like something your mum might say, but it's true. Pull those shoulders back and move like you're proud of who you are, soon enough you'll actually feel it too.

2. Become an art girl and take some moody pictures with your camera, join a trampoline class or become a superchef – whatever you choose make sure it's something you've never done before.

3. Think good thoughts. When you're feeling a little bit nervy, remember good times for an instant boost.

4. Be nice to yourself. You'll be hanging out with yourself for a long time so you'd better kiss and make up.

5. Smile. A lot.

How to...Go ahead!

I used to have one of those fabulously fab-like Magic 8 Balls, a destiny-deciding device that is ever so helpful when you're as indecisive a person as moi...thing is, the ball didn't always tell me what I wanted to hear so I decided to make me some sassy 'Go Ahead' cards to keep in my Think Pink vanity case. These sparkly-gorgeous little cards give me permission to do something I love every day – how cool?!

Directions:
1. Take a big piece of card and cut it into 10 sections
2. On each section draw or write something you would love to do
3. Place your set of cards in a bowl or bag
4. Close your eyes and pick one
5. Say after me...'Go ahead and....'

What you will need:
✯ Card ✯ Colouring in facilities
✯ Scissors

If you need any ideas, here are mine:
Wear false eyelashes...Take a nap... Beautify from head to toe...Play air guitar...Emulate the style of a 50's pin-up girl...Shop...Read a book... Paint the town pink...

Shine like a star!

To shine like the superstar sparkle girl you truly are, take a tip from those celeb types.

★ Wear shades at all times – pink, natch – the world is a truly amazing place when seen through these.

★ Get a look that's all yours – you need a look that's completely YOU-nique for your moment in the limelight.

★ Be determined. Celeb types don't give up when life gets a little real-lifey and seeing as that's what you are, nor should you lil' missy.

★ Accept compliments – when someone says how fabulous you look, be sure to thank them right back coz rejecting a compliment is super rude. Don't question the person's obvious good taste and judgement – I make a habit of collecting candy-kissed compliments, you should too!

★ Bag a buff boy – it's not essential but c'mon, a boytoy to walk down the red carpet with would be rather nice, wouldn't it? I like the shaggy-haired guitar boys but there are so many kinds of yummy boy-shaped candy: Sporty-yet-sensitive-jock boys, deep-and-meaningful-book boys and cute-and-quiet-boy-next door boys, the list goes on...

Hey Good Lookin'!

'...DON'T WAIT FOR OTHERS TO TREAT YOU LIKE THE PRINCESS YOU UNDOUBTEDLY ARE...'

I'm feisty, fun, fearless and fabulous.

FACT.

How do I know? Because I tell myself everyday.

I've got a chubby tummy and hair that doesn't do what it should but, inside, I know I'm sunshine and smiles and deserve to be treated like a punk-prom princess. So instead of running from my reflection, I just tell myself how sparkly-gorgeous I am as many times as it takes for me to actually believe it.

90% of chicas spend their time fretting about parts of their body that they don't like. Most of these hang-ups are based on what we think we should look like, according to the media and celeb types.

Now listen up, images in a magazine are airbrushed and manipulated to become Polaroids of perfection. While celeb types have a whole entourage of stylists, make up artists, and wardrobe people to make sure they're looking tip-top and tooti-frutti at all times - they're not true representations of us chicas. We come in all different shapes and sizes and are all totally YOU-nique.

When you Think Pink constant comparisons to Britney, Beyonce or any other pop diva beginning with 'B' for that matter, are banished. Instead they are replaced with a super-cool mantra that will make sure you feel like a star-shaped, sunshine girl at all times, mine's 'There's only one me. And I rock!'

What's yours going to be?

....

....

....

....

....

....

Notes:

....
....
....
....
....
....
....
....
....
....
....
....
....
....
....
....
....
....
....
....
....
....
....
....
....
....
....
....
....
....
....
....
....
....
....
....

Looking Good?

Do you smile when you look in the mirror or do you want to run in the opposite direction?

You go shopping with your mates and they're all trying on clothes, do you:
a. watch but don't join in because you'd look awful in everything
b. try everything on too, it'll be great fun!

You sleep through your alarm and have to get ready in a rush. Before leaving the house you take one final look at yourself, do you:
a. burst into tears at your reflection and search for a paper bag to put over your head
b. pull your hair back, dab on some lip gloss and smile

You're watching MTV when they introduce a new girl group do you:
a. instantly compare yourself to them and realise they've got skinnier legs, a smaller tummy and glossier hair than you
b. turn your nose up at the music but love the cut-off denim skirt the lead singer is wearing

You're at a party throwing some serious shapes on the dance floor when you notice a group of girls looking over, do you:
a. stop immediately and blush with embarrassment
b. smile at them safe in the knowledge that they're lovin' the moves that you're bustin'

When you get home, you can hardly contain your yawns do you:
a. lay awake thinking about how great everyone else looked
b. clean off your make up and fall straight to sleep, you're so tired after all that dancing!

Mostly a's:

Too much time spent comparing yourself to others and worrying about what other people think of you means that life becomes all sorts of dull. Try not to compare yourselves to anyone, you're YOU-nique. Next time you look in the mirror, I dare you to find at least one thing you like about yourself, it can be your oh-so-long eyelashes that don't need mascara, the way your favourite jeans hug your bum, the sprinkling of freckles across your nose, just something that when you look in the mirror turns your frown upside down!

Mostly b's:

You know that nobody is perfect so instead of getting hung up on the bits you don't like, you celebrate and enhance the good stuff. There are even times when you embrace the not-so-good bits anyway, because you know that when it all comes together, it makes a super cool version of YOU and that's such a good thing.

No Comparison

My very cool and prettilicious friend, Sadie, thinks that her life would be infinitely more fabulous if she had bigger lady bumps. She obsesses about her 34A bra fillers on a daily basis, expressing the need and necessity for plastic surgery as soon as she turns 16, to anyone who will listen. Today is no exception.

'It's not fair,' she says, with her hands on her T-shirt covered chest, standing in front of my full-length, fairy light-lit, bedroom mirror. 'Why haven't I got boobs like Eva Satine?'

While others may pick up glossy magazines and go green with envy at images of models, actresses and celeb types, the object of obsession at our school is Evil Eva. She's that girl. The one who's beautifully packaged but has nasty, knotted insides that make her very rude and terribly unpretty.

Despite this, Sadie wants to be her, a lot.

Not because she gets good grades (which she does), or because she's got teeth like a girl out of a toothpaste commercial (which she has), no, it's because she has, according to Sadie, the perfect cleavage.

'They're just so round and, you know, there,' gestures Sadie pushing her own lady bumps together and upwards.

I sigh a big sigh. I've never wanted big boobs but I did used to wonder what it would be like to be a size 10 or to have a walk-in wardrobe like Eva, but when I saw the world through pink-tinted shades I realised how super-boring it would be if we were all the same. We'd be like a teen version of The Stepford Wives, all glossy hair and robot-like with false smiles and no personality. That would most definitely not rock.

I give Sadie the hugest hug, and tell her that she is the most scrumptiously gorgeous girl and that having a small chest is cool because she gets to wear those to-die-for tight tees from the kids department that cost £2.99. She nudges me playfully in the ribs, before breaking into a fit of giggles. She agrees that this is most deffo a good reason and one that she hadn't previously thought of. I then tell her how much the average bra costs and she is even more than thankful that she doesn't have to wear one yet.

Change what you see

Take a look in the mirror, I know it might sound a bit scary but for every so-called imperfection you find, instead of feeling bad and sad about it, change it into a positively smile-worthy thing. It's simple...

BEFORE: 'I've got so many freckles, I hate them.'
AFTER: 'Having freckles will always mean I look younger than I am, which will be very helpful when I'm 84.'

BEFORE: 'I have to wear glasses all the time'
AFTER: 'Wearing glasses will mean I no longer miss out on a buff-beauty stealing glances – I will also look super smart!'

Your turn!

BEFORE:..
....
....
AFTER:..
....
....

BEFORE:..
....
....
AFTER:..
....
....

This girl will rock your world...
The lovely Lauren Laverne – radio DJ, TV presenter, guitar strumming goddess, queen of cool – rock on!

She says: 'IT'S REALLY TOUGH BEING A TEENAGER AND GIRLS ARE SO HARD ON THEMSELVES, BUT IT DOES GET BETTER. JUST BE NICE TO YOURSELF. YOU'RE THE MOST IMPORTANT PERSON IN YOUR LIFE SO BE HAPPY AND ENJOY YOURSELF.'

Dare to be different

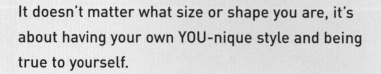

It doesn't matter what size or shape you are, it's about having your own YOU-nique style and being true to yourself.

I rip up any rulebook that tells me what I should or shouldn't wear because life is far too short to conform. We all have different sides to our personalities – that's what makes us so distinctive and interesting. So what if one day you want to be all 1950s glam girl and the next you want to be a retro punk princess?

While these contradictions might be confusing to others, they are the things that make you individual so make sure you hug them up because, where style is concerned, there really are no rules. It doesn't matter what size or shape you are, it's about having your own YOU-nique style and being true to yourself. Think Pink, princess, and set your own trends. Work on the principle that whether it's this season or football season, style is not about rules, it's about the endless possibilities.

Of course there is a chance this can lead to serious fashion faux pas territory, like the time I thought it would be super cool to let trainee hairdresser and guitar playing pink lady, Bella, cut my fringe with her Hello Kitty scissors. I ended up with an oh-so-short, asymmetric 'thing'. As you can imagine, it wasn't my finest fashion moment but, with a few v.cute sparkly hair slides I managed to flip it into a moment to shine, because the next day people were commenting on how cool it looked!

This proves you never know unless you give it a go, with a little imagination I managed to transform what was just a wonky fringe into a look that was too-cool-for-school!

Be Experimental

Don't be afraid to experiment and find out what works for you. Experimenting with my appearance is my absolute favourite thing to do. Whether it's trying out the latest fluro-green eyeshadow or adding a whole lot of sequin-sparkle to an old pair of jeans, experimenting is my playground! Vintage finds, homemade punk-trash trinkets and oh-so-kitsch ensembles scatter every corner of my room making it a sparkly-gorgeous treasure chest for any would-be customising queen.

Customising is the coolest, there's no better way to express yourself and show what you're all about than by making your clothes and accessories a reflection of your personality. Prettify your belongings by letting your imagination run wild. If your creativity needs a kickstart, take a look inside the Think Pink vanity case to find all you need to run riot with your wardrobe...

Custom-made

What you need:
A case/box: I use a mini pink vanity case to keep my customising kit all in one place
Fabric glue: If sewing doesn't float your boat then this is a great way of sticking material like too cute patches on your jeans
Fabric paints: Simply the coolest way of creating super fun designs on tiny tees
Scissors: Embroidery scissors are most deffo the way forward for chopping material, but if you can't get your hands on any, then kitchen scissors will do.
Superglue: If you're making jewellery or sticking pieces that can't be sewn this is super strong. Just be sure not to stick your manicured fingers together in the process!
Sewing stuff: An assortment of needles and threads because stitchin' is officially bitchin'!

Start simple with designing a cute tee, then as you begin to gain confidence and have endless ideas, let your imagination run wild. My favourite thing is to go round charity shops searching for cool one-offs, don't just look for clothes, I like to find sparkly buttons that I could add to a plain old shirt – the possibilities are endless, chica!

Prettify your belongings
by letting your imagination
run wild.

This girl will rock your world...

Leona Baker, queen of super cool label, Lady Luck - pop art jewellery for music-junkie-fashion-freaks, has made customising her living and is now receiving major press coverage from here to LA.

She says...

"I WORKED AS AN ASSISTANT STYLIST ON POP VIDEOS AND FASHION SHOOTS AND SOLD CUTE FINDS AT PORTOBELLO MARKET ON SATURDAYS. I DISLIKED THE FASHION HIERARCHY AND WANTED TO DO MY OWN THING. AS I ENJOYED SOURCING AND MAKING STUFF TO SELL ON MY STALL SO MUCH, I TURNED IT INTO A FULL TIME THING AND BOUGHT MY PITCH AT PORTOBELLO MARKET, LONDON.

I LIKE SEEING KOOKY GIRLS DO THE HOLLYWOOD THING, LIKE CHLOE SEVIGNY, MAGGIE GYLLENHAAL AND KIRSTEN DUNST.

Leona's tips for would-be customisers:

"...HAVE AN OPEN MIND WHEN LOOKING FOR STUFF TO CUSTOMISE WITH. YOUR LOCAL CRAFT SHOP MIGHT LOOK LIKE IT'S FOR GRANNIES, BUT THERE'S ALWAYS A CHANCE THEY'LL HAVE A STASH OF 1980'S PATCHES IN THE BASEMENT. LEARN THE NAMES OF THE PEOPLE WHO WORK IN YOUR LOCAL CHARITY SHOP, TELL THEM WHAT YOU'RE LOOKING FOR AND THEY MIGHT START PUTTING THINGS ASIDE FOR YOU! IF YOU DON'T LIKE EARLY MORNINGS (I'M ALWAYS THE FIRST TO TURN UP AT A CAR BOOT SALE!), EBAY IS A GREAT WAY TO THRIFT IN YOUR ARM CHAIR. LOG YOUR DETAILS INTO 'MY EBAY' AND YOU CAN TYPE IN ALL YOUR FAVE SEARCH WORDS AND THEY WILL E-MAIL YOU WHEN SOMETHING IS LISTED THAT MATCHES YOUR DESCRIPTION. SOME OF MY KEYWORDS ARE '80'S CHARMS', 'BAMBI' AND 'BLONDIE BADGES'! GOOD LUCK FELLOW CUSTOMISING QUEENS!..."

www.ladyluckrulesok.com

super cool postcards to send to friends

POP ROCKER *Necklace*

ALSO AVAILABLE:
NEW YORK DOLLS,
RAMONES,
JOAN JETT,
KISS

New York Dolls

GO-GO GUITARS
AVAILABLE IN 6 STYLES!

my ladyluckrules accessories rock

Be inspired!

It would be easy to let those media and celeb types decide what we should look like and what we should wear but when you're lovin' the skin you're in, you don't need to compare yourselves to them, instead, look to them for inspiration.

Leading ladies who I love are:
Audrey Hepburn – stylish, chic and simply divine, Gwen Stefani – the woman is so damn cool it hurts with her red lips, vintage ensembles and an amazing ability to accessorise, Kelly Osbourne – unconventional, kooky and oozing attitude and, of course, the lovely Lauren Laverne – guitar playing, silver-tounged blonde-haired beauty who's not afraid to experiment.

They're all completely different in appearance and I'm never going to look like any of them, but that doesn't stop me rocking their style to maximum effect.

Whose style do you adore and why?

....

....

....

....

....

....

....

....

....

....

....

....

....

....

....

....

....

....

....

....
....
....
....
....
....
....

How would you dress if you didn't care what people thought?

....
....
....
....
....
....
....
....
....
....
....
....
....
....
....
....
....
....
....
....
....
....
....
....
....
....
....
....

Try this:
Before deciding on how things should look, magazine editor types create a 'mood board'. They cut and paste all the things they like and are inspired by: colours, fabrics, hairstyles, people, etc. to create a super-cool collage of ideas. Not only does it look cool it is a great way to generate themes and styles. Surf the internet or go to your local library and make a mood board of all your favourite styles from the past right through to now, make a note of what you like so much about each one and then borrow from different eras and icons to create your own sparkly-gorgeous look.

How to work... The Audrey Look

Audrey Hepburn is one of my all time favourite leading ladies, check me out working my very own 'Audrey look' with a modern day spin...

Under pressure

It's all too easy to feel pressurised by the media and get sucked into the narrow-minded stereotypical image of how you should look. But take a look around you. How many of us actually look like the size eight models that we see in magazines? The answer? Not many. So why don't teen mags use real girls who represent us? A teen journo lady explains.

"...the sample sizes that we get from the fashion companies are model-sizes which makes it tricky to do shoots with plus-sized models but we are very strict that the models we use in our fashion and beauty pages look healthy..."

you're lovely chica, smile!...

Lola's 'love yourself' rules

Beauty is the stuff that goes on inside and shines outward, the sparkle in your eyes, your smile, your attitude. You are an exclusive, one-of-a-kind package, with your own unique selling points so be sure to celebrate them, gorgeous girl!

★ Being thin does not make you perfect - it's more important to be healthy than to be thin. So ditch any ideas of diets, eat healthily and be a water babe and drink eight glasses of water a day.

★ Whether it's singing into a hairbrush, making jewellery, writing a book, find something you love hugely and indulge yourself.

★ Enjoy being yourself and sunbathe in all your kick-ass qualities as well as your quirky, kooky awkward ways.

★ Look into the mirror every morning and tell yourself how amazing you are, even if you've got last night's mascara smudged down one cheek and your hair is reminiscent of Cameron Diaz in 'Something About Mary'.

★ Make no comparisons – you are you and you rock – so there!

it's a girl thing

'IT'S BETTER TO LOSE AN ARGUMENT THAN TO LOSE A FRIEND.'

'CHICK FLICKS, BOY TALK AND CONSUMING A COPIOUS AMOUNT OF CHOCOLATE WITH YOUR GIGGLE GIRLS...PRICELESS.'

They say that diamonds are a girl's best friend and yes, while I am a big fan of all things sparkly-gorgeous, diamonds can't give you a hug when you're feeling sad, they can't make you laugh out loud when you're really not supposed to and they can't eat an entire vat of chocolate in one sitting now, can they?

How do you rate as a mate?

....
....
....
....
....
....
....
....
....
....
....
....
....

What kind of friend are you?

....
....
....
....
....
....
....
....
....
....
....
....
....

Your best mate has had yet another row with her guy, do you:

a. Tell her you'll call her back when The OC has finished

b. You're already on your way round to hers with an industrial sized bar of chocolate

Your friend is struggling with her science revision – a subject you rock at, do you:

a. Suggest she'd find it much easier to revise if she gave up her part time job

b. Offer to tutor her for an afternoon

Your boy bud has invited you and your girls to a party. The thing is, his best mate recently broke one of your friend's hearts – boo. Do you:

a. Tell her to get over it, you don't want to miss the chance of being seen at the coolest party ever

b. Apologise to your boy bud for not going to his party and go to the cinema with your broken hearted gal pal instead

Your friend is having a first-date fashion 'moment' and rings to ask if she can borrow your brand new, not ever been worn sparkly mules, do you:

a. Lie and say that your sister has borrowed them, there's no way someone is going to get to wear them before you

b. Sigh a big sigh, pretend to think about it before telling her to come round when she's finished putting her make-up on, of course she can borrow them, this is a first date emergency after all!

The parents that you babysit for have been super-generous this week, do you:

a. Buy yourself a gorgeous pair of boots

b. Treat all your friends to a slice of gooey chocolate cake

Mostly a's:

You're one of those to-the-point type friends who think 'being cruel to be kind' is a do-able option. But there's a fine line between helpful insight and hard-to-take harshness. Perhaps you've been hurt by a friend in the past or been taken for granted, but making friendships work is all about give and take and being thoughtful – go on, try it!

Mostly b's:

You're one special friend, you're well-balanced, un-jealous, warm and great company. Your giggle girls love you and know they can count on you without treating you like a doormat – will you be my friend too please?

These girls will rock your world...

Let me introduce you to my feisty, fun, fearless and fabulous very own version of The Pink Ladies...Angel, Bella and Sadie – lipgloss laden, secret sharing, chocolate eating, giggle girls. They're my bestest friends who I wouldn't swap for any amount of diamonds, not ever!

Me, Lola!

My obsession with movies and stars of the silver screen combined with a love of pampering means that I am truly fabulous, sweetie! My life is filled with thousands of candy-kissed moments because I'm in control. I make the rules, I'm both the director and the leading lady of my super cool movie and I'm determined to make my life totally A- List!

Three most listened to tracks on my mp3 player:
The Kinks – Lola
Kym Mazelle – Young Hearts Run Free
Irene Cara – What a Feeling/Flashdance
(What can I say? I'm having an 80s phase!)
Why I rock:
(according to Bella, Sadie and Angel...) She's got pink hair, she makes us laugh so much that we snort pink lemonade through our noses, she's the best listener, gives great advice and she inspires us to live life to the fullest – she's just fabulous personified! Ah shux!

Angel

Angel is my best friend in the entire world. She holds the key to a treasure chest of crushes, dreams and stuff my parentals will never, ever know. She is a dedicated follower of fashion, with the biggest afro you are ever likely to see in your entire life. She is a fashionista of the highest order worshiping at the throne of all that is glossy and magazine-like. She buys every magazine the day it hits the shop shelves and is working the entire contents of its fashion and beauty pages by 6pm the same day.

Three most listened to tracks on Angel's mp3 player:
Aretha Franklin – Respect
Amy Winehouse – Stronger Than Me
Jill Sobule –Supermodel
Why she rocks:
She is a no-nonsense kinda girl, busting with sassy 'tude and determination - I love her!

Sadie

Sadie is a real fun-time-frankee and ensures our social calendar is permanently full-to-the-brim with cool things to do. She'll never let anyone or anything rain on her sparkly-pink parade. Get this, we'd been planning to go to a festival all year but Angel's parentals became all parent-like and said she couldn't go, so instead of stomping her cute lil' ballet pumps and getting all mad, mad, mad, Sadie organised 'Pink Fest' in her back garden...She pitched an oh-so-cute pink tent filled with all kinds of pink treats like candyfloss and pink lemonade, we all had to wear pink (natch) and she used her superstar DJ skills to mix a compilation CD of all our favourite grrrl tunes to rock out to!

Three most listened to tracks on Sadie's mp3 player:
The Donnas – Friends Like Mine
The Thrills – Big Sur
Lucky Star – Madonna
Why she rocks:
She always sees the best in people and has a smile that is simply infectious!

Bella

Bella rocks my world, she's three years older than me, lives next door and is the ultimate go-for-it girl willing to give anything a go once. Having moved here from America last summer, I remember being completely awestruck by her effortless cool. She pulled out a bright pink Daisy Rock heart-shaped guitar from the back of a VW camper van and carried it under her elaborately illustrated arm. I just knew I had to know her. I was right.

Three most listened to tracks on Bella's mp3 player:
Hole – Reasons to be Beautiful
Blondie – Heart of Glass
Tuuli Rockstar – Potential
Why she rocks:
She's trashy, punk rock chic in laddered fishnet tights and is the queen of storytelling having travelled the world with her boho parentals. She's not afraid of anything, not even spiders, and she has taught me to play three chords on the gee-tar; well that's all you need to make a hit record these days isn't it? Bella rocks – literally.

Mates are great

The Pink Ladies are all so very different, yet we complement each other like the perfect pink tote bag and peep-toe shoe combination. Thankfully, we're nothing like the ego driven clique 'The laydeebitches.' Pronounced 'laydee – bishay' and to be said in a French accent (we were going through our 'we heart all things continental' phase when we named evil Eva Satine's hair-swinging-gum-smacking girl gang and the more-than-apt title kinda stuck). These girls currently rule the school.

sadie

lola

Sadie and I are the only Pink Ladies who attend Parkfield comp and consequently are probably the only two people who do not want to be part of their crew. Don't get me wrong, I can more than see the attraction, these girls are seriously glam, they spend an entirety obsessing over their just-stepped-out-of-a-salon locks, checking mirrors and monitoring the need for gloss application on a five minute basis.

Thing is, this constant quest for perfection is not about enhancing their own qualities, it's based solely on becoming a carbon copy of evil Eva. These girls are so insecure that they have no interest in being the gorgeous sparkle girls they could be and instead would rather make other people feel bad with the never-ending supply of put-downs and cuss words that are part of their everyday vocab – boo.

Sadie and I feel sorry for them.

No, really we do, because life must be super tough for them... Think about it, the Pink Ladies appreciate what we add to each other's lives - we learn from each other, support each other, give glitter-filled hugs on a daily basis, run up ridiculously huge phone bills at the expense of our parentals when we've seen each other at school all day, but most importantly, we get each other, like, really get each other and celebrate each others' quirky, awkward ways because they're the things that make us special.

By being so self-obsessed and having an image of so-called perfection to uphold, The Laydeebitches must be under so much pressure to live up to their reputation. Plus, they're missing out on hanging with friends who have a cheery outlook and who can see the fun and potential in everyone and everything. Now that, to me, is all sorts of sad.

List all your very best friends:

....

....

....

....

....

....

....

....

....

....

....

....

....

....

List all the reasons why they rock your world:

....

....

....

....

....

....

....

....

....

....

....

....

....

....

....

....

Being a kick-ass friend – the rules

In order to have amazing friends, you have to actually be a friend, these are the Pink Ladies' friendship rules – what are yours?

☆ We love to share our secrets, especially about who's crushing on who but, in order to be trusted as a fantastic friend, they need to be kept.

☆ If you make a promise, stick to it. Going back on your word only makes you feel guilty and will destroy your friend's trust. Be the kind of girl that really means what she says.

...be loyal, don't betray them and never forget them...

☆ To always be there even when the good times aren't – the fun times are fab and laughing is one of our favourite things to do, but there are going to be times when life gets a little bit sucky and a shoulder is most deffo needed to cry on, sometimes all we need is a supportive listener, someone who isn't going to judge us or interrupt us.

☆ It's a great feeling when somebody loves you just for being you, so celebrate your differences and learn from each other's experiences...For example, Bella has introduced us to a whole new music scene, Sadie has taught us how to write Haiku (v.cool poetry, wanna try? Turn to page 191) Angel has made sure we can apply lipstick without turning into a scary Mary and I host 'Film Friday' every week, an evening of celluloid nostalgia educating the Pink Ladies in all that is great and good in cinema...

☆ Last but not least, be loyal, don't betray them and never forget them even when you're a guitar playin', glitter girl in a chart topping rock band, playing gigs all over the world and surrounded by shaggy haired, rock boys – mmmm...

The Pink Ladies are proof that you don't have to look alike or necessarily share all of the same interests to be the best of friends, just make sure you treat your mates how you'd like to be treated yourself and you'll be well on the way to being best bud material.

Peer pressure

Being popular and fitting in might seem like they should be mucho important, but I've discovered that they're really not. Unless you're completely happy with the star-shine glitter girl that you are, then you're always going to feel like you want to be someone or someplace else.

Last year, before I met Sadie, a few of The Laydeebitches asked me to cut class with them. I said yes because I was super desperate to fit in and I thought this was my one chance at finally being accepted. The funny thing was, once we negotiated our way past the school gates, no one really knew what to do next except sit on the playing field and smoke. This is where my plan to become part of the cool crew came unstuck. They asked me to give it a go, but smoking is for losers and there was no way I was going to smell like an upturned ashtray and give myself premature wrinkles just for the chance of hanging with their crew.

...it's super tough to be the only one who says 'no' to peer pressure, you can do it.

At the risk of ridicule, I politely declined. Needless to say they went on to ignore me for the rest of term, but if you believe in something the way I believe that smoking is icky and wrong, you've got to stand by it no matter what. For sure, I wanted to be popular but not enough that I would risk my health and rosy pink complexion in the process.

So whether it's the popular girls asking you to try a cigarette, your netball friend trying to convince you to be mean to another player and never pass her the ball, or a girl in your street asking you to shoplift for her, Think Pink and you'll realise that although it's tough to be the only one who says 'no' to peer pressure, you can do it.

✩ Pay attention to your own feelings and beliefs about what is right and wrong in your glitter-filled world and stay true to that.

✩ Avoid toxic types – you know who they are, they might be part of the cool crew but you wouldn't want them as a friend, would you?

✩ Knowing yourself really well and being happy with who you are will stop you from being tempted to do something to please others or to fit in.

✩ Be strong and just walk away.

Pal potential

I used to be a bit of a misfit, I didn't feel like I fitted in anywhere, my only friend was Angel and she was at a posh boarding school a gazillion miles away. There were people who I thought looked cool, but I was far too shy to approach them and then there were people like The Ladybitches who I did my best to avoid at all costs.

This meant I became a bit of a loner, with just my Audrey Hepburn DVD collection and a pink, leather bound journal for company. That was okay for a while as 'Lola time' is mucho important, but it wasn't until I saw the world through my pink-tinted shades that I also saw how cool it would be to have friends who I could spend time with creating adventures and exploring new things.

...it wasn't until I started seeing all my kooky, awkward ways as things that make me cool, that I realised others might too.

So what stopped me?

Well, nothing, apart from the fact I was painfully shy and thought there was no one out there who would ever actually 'get' me.

How wrong could one chica be?

You see, it wasn't until I started seeing all my kooky, awkward ways as things that make me cool, that I realised others might too.

If you don't have your own version of the Pink Ladies yet, or if you already have great friends but would like to make new ones, (because let's face it, you can never have too many) you need to Think Pink, chica...

Why would you be a super cool mate to have?

....

....

....

....

....

....

....

....

....

....

List all the qualities you look for in a bestie:

....

....

....

....

....

....

....

....

....

....

How to... Make new friends

...meet new people outside of class - join an after-school club.

You know that really cool girl who everyone wants to hang out with because she's always smiling and having fun? Well say goodbye to lil' miss shy and that could be you with a pinch of self-confidence, lots of smiles and an interest in others...

☆ Don't interrupt a conversation, but if you hear someone talking about your favourite band or a film you've seen, don't be afraid to show an interest and offer a new perspective.

☆ The only people you're going to meet sat in front of the TV each night are the cast of your favourite soap, so to meet new people outside of class join an after-school club. Whether you're a Sportstar Susie or Artgirl Amy there's guaranteed to be something at school or your local youth centre that will float your boat, you'll get to learn new skills with the added bonus of hanging with people who have similar interests as you.

☆ If someone is wearing a pair of shoes that you adore mostest, tell them that you're digging their footwear and was wondering where they got them from, not only will the person be super flattered, they'll also know you're a chica of impeccable taste who they will want to be friends with.

☆ Make sure that when you speak to someone for the first time you don't spend the whole conversation talking about you. Without being super nosey, ask them questions about themselves, I love finding out about people and their lives, it's half the fun of making new friends.

☆ Most importantly, don't dump your old friends when new ones come on the scene. Angel was my only friend and she's very different to Bella and Sadie so I made sure to introduce them all, it took a while for everyone to get to know each other, but eventually everyone was hanging out at mine and we officially became the Pink Ladies – coolio.

Girl-bonding

Sleepovers are my most favourite way to girl-bond. They give you and your gal pals chance to hang out without a deadline and to indulge in chocolate eating, secret sharing, game playing and film watching in no particular order...

I've combined my love of friends, sleepovers and films and declared every Friday at my house 'Film Friday.' We all take turns in choosing a film and dress up accordingly. Mine's generally old school movies starring glamour queens from the 50's and 60's who are all so beautiful they make my breath stop, which means I get to wear my too-cute, pale pink prom dress and watch 'Gentlemen Prefer Blondes' with Marilyn Monroe. After the film we change into our comfies and alternate between a board game bonanza and a beauty bash which normally involves lashing substantial amounts of mashed banana over our faces in a bid to combat pimples.

Oh my stars, I love Fridays!

Film Friday favourites
Dirty Dancing – because *nobody* puts Baby in the corner.
Almost Famous – not only is it a kick-ass film, it's a great opportunity to be completely inspired by Kate Hudson's countless chic ensembles.
Anything with Audrey Hepburn – just because...
Ghost World – don't worry, it's not scary, just two kooky girls and the weird and wonderful world that is their life – we heart Ghost World. A lot.
Amelie – She's French, she's a magic girl and she's a complete dollface – j'adore Amelie mostest.
Clueless – for everyone who's ever worn a dress by a 'very important' designer.

acting out my fave film!

How to...throw your own slumber party

Introducing the Think Pink Pyjama Party kit!

What you will need:
- ★ To get the all clear from the Parentals
- ★ Invites – don't just send a text, make it a proper event, letting them know your theme and what you would like them to wear.
- ★ Have a plan of action: Rent the DVDs, plan your 'theme' outfit, and provide some munchies - combine a substantial amount of chocolate with some healthier options.
- ★ Some pink card to make your game board

Directions:
- ★ Have mucho fun!
- ★ Drink pink lemonade – well, why not?
- ★ Turn the page to play the Think Pink board game, it's hours of feel good fun because lets face it, girl-bonding rocks!

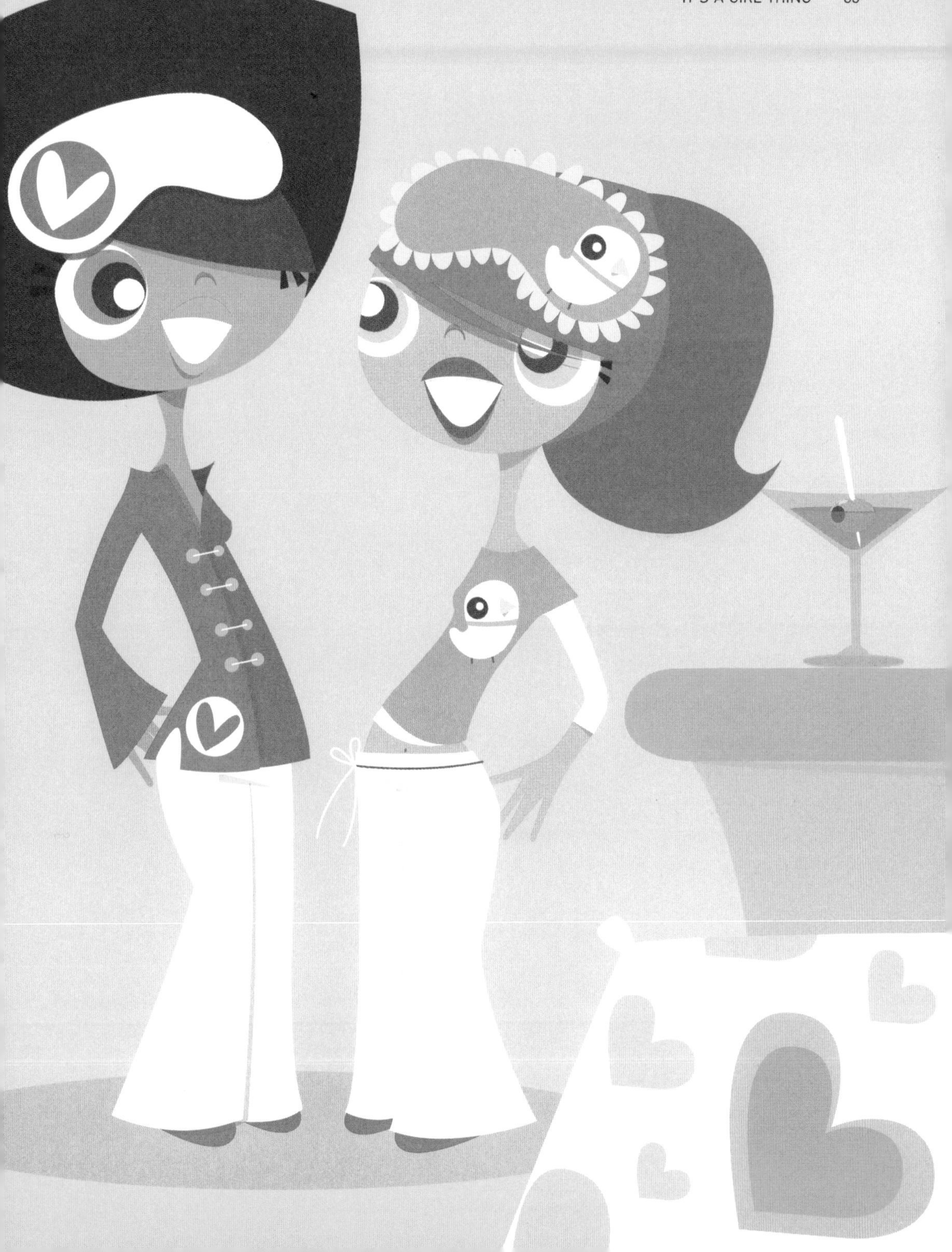

Think Pink – The Game

A magic carpet ride of self-discovery to be taken with your giggle girls as often as possible!

What you will need:
* ★ Your comfies – pj's, slippers, whatever makes you feel warm and fuzzy
* ★ A dice – unfortunately not provided, so may I suggest you borrow one from a simply less interesting board game
* ★ Paper and pen – to record your answers
* ★ Coloured smarties – these will be used as counters with the added bonus that you can eat them straight after!

Directions:
* ★ Choose a coloured smartie and place it on 'start'.
* ★ The numbers on the dice represent an instruction, roll the dice and match the number you have rolled with the instruction.

Instructions:
1 = Sing a line from your favourite song and move 2 places
2 = Invent a new dance move and move 1 place
3 = Chill your boots, chica – miss a turn
4 = Give yourself a new nickname and move 2 places
5 = Pout like a movie star and move 1 place
6 = Eat some chocolate while you miss a go

The Fall Out

Sometimes even the best of friends fall out. Angel and I have always argued over the silliest of things, everything from boys to film endings. But luckily we can never stay mad at each other for too long and end up laughing so hard we get headaches and want to pee. But real arguments can be all sorts of sucky, they can leave us feeling sad and mad and unsure of what to do next. In order to get things back on track you need to Think Pink...

It's good to talk

The most mucho important thing is to get talking again. You need to talk it through, come to an agreement without it all turning into another messy argument. So, take deep breaths, be calm and tactful, let her know how you feel and then listen to what she has to say.

Don't get mad

Try not to get angry, count to ten before you say anything. That way you won't say anything you later wish you hadn't.

'Fess up

Think about the argument for a minute. Who is really to blame here? If it was you, be brave, accept that your friend has every reason to be mad at you, listen to what she has to say and then apologise. A chocolate bar may also aid this particular process.

Be a compromise queen

If the argument is about the two of you wanting to do different things, instead of you both getting all stressy, try and find some middle ground you're both happy with.

Agree to disgree

Just coz you're BFF doesn't mean you're gonna always agree, so instead of prolonging an argument and wasting valuable girl-bonding time sulking, just agree to disagree, it really is that simple!

If all else fails, resort to the motto I keep in the Think Pink vanity case: 'IT'S BETTER TO LOSE AN ARGUMENT THAN TO LOSE A FRIEND.'

Mad about the boy

'...THEY WILL BREAK YOUR HEART AT A HUNDRED PACES... BUT THEY ARE BEAUTIFUL...'

Believe it or not, bagging a buff boy is not of mucho importance in my life right now. I've got a gazillion other things to focus on, like my schoolwork, having fun with my Pink Ladies and making sure I spend valuable time with myself becoming the best star shine girl I can possibly be.

This does not, however, mean that I do not like boys, because, j 'adore boys mostest. In fact, appreciating the boy form and honing my eyelash fluttering, skirty-flirty skills are by far my one of most preferred and favourite wastes of time!

Are you baffled by boys or are you clued up when it comes to those boy types?

You're walking your pet pooch when a group of boys kick a ball in your direction, do you:
a. Think they're picking on you and walk in the opposite direction.
b. Assume that one of them is digging on you and smile.

Your bestie tells you that a buff boy in class is crushin' on you, do you:
a. Think she's winding you up.
b. Do a celebration dance and ask her advice what she thinks you should do next.

Your crush has invited you to his birthday party, do you:
a. Decide not to go and put a card through his door instead.
b. Turn up looking fabulous and hand him a CD you just know he'll love.

You've hit the shops with your giggle girls when a dude you vaguely recognise asks for you mobile number, do you:
a. Make your apologies, it's obvious that he's mistaken you for someone else.
b. Feel totally flattered, but ask him for his instead, you don't give your number out to just anyone.

Your best mate has just popped to the shop to get chocolate supplies leaving you alone with her older bro, do you:

a. Turn bright red and get totally tongue-tied.
b. Ask him if he wants to play Grand Theft Auto on the PS2.

Mostly a's

Boys most definitely baffle you, don't they? No worries though, because you're not alone. Those boy types are a bit of a mystery and most girls will admit they find lads little habits a bit strange. Believe it or not, they do have some cool qualities and can be all sorts of fun so don't be afraid to hang out with them and get to know them.

Mostly b's

You're completely cool with boys and their behaviour and feel totally at ease in their company, I'm jealous! You're so chilled out around boys that you're more than cool with showing you can be 'one of the lads' as well as a potential date – you're boy sussed, sista!

Boy world

...life is just that little bit sweeter when you're crazy in crush with a boy...

Admittedly, I've only really been interested in boy types for the past year or so, but in that year I think I've managed to put together a pretty clear picture of the whole boy set up. Y'see, I've figured that whoever said that boy types were from Mars was not only suggesting they were from another planet (which they most deffo are) but was also referring to the chocolate factory in which Mars bars are produced, because, to me, boy world is just like a yummy, melt-in-the-mouth bar of chocolate - stick with me on this one...

✩ Chocolates come in an assortment of shapes and sizes – as do boys. Fact.

✩ Some are beautifully wrapped while others are cheaply packaged but they're still equally as yummy – think trendy jock type and emo rock boy, both are very different in style, but equally as cute.

✩ Some have hard exteriors with a super soft centre – y'know the type, they'll act super hard in front of their mates but when they're with you they will be all sugar-coated cuteness.

✩ They can be bad for us if consumed on a regular basis – if we spend all our time with dream dude, our marks slip and our friends forget our name.

✩ Some are like a coffee crème, they look nice, you think you're going to like them, but in fact they make you feel slightly icky – sometimes we think we like someone based on their looks alone, but it's not until we get to know them that we realise they're not nice. Not one little bit.

One thing's for sure though, there's no denying it, life is just that little bit sweeter when you're crazy in crush with a boy type.

Boy Crushing

If ever an excuse was needed to waste time, crushing on boys would be it. Until a couple of weeks ago I was crushing on the too-cute Jake Farrell. He is all square of jaw and twinkly of eye and until I had the unpleasant experience of spending time with him, I thought he was a strawberry milkshake with chocolate sprinkles - yum.

Turns out he wasn't.

Turns out he was an icky, man-made fibre wearing, jock-ass. Boo. But that's why crushing is so cool because unlike real boyfriends, a crush isn't a real boy. He's everything you want him to be, not actually what he is. Y'see, I had painted this too-good-to-be-true version of Jake, he came in the sports jock package, but inside, he had the warmest of hearts. He would feed me chocolate and open doors for me. He would read poetry and we would have cool conversations about art and films under the stars. In reality however, Jake was a bit letchy, liked football and copied my maths homework.

...let's face it, boys are just nice to look at.

Which is why I reckon boy crushing should stay just that for now. A crush. That way the object of your affection is more inclined to sit happily on the pedestal you've put him on. He'll always look his best, you won't ever need to know about his nasty habits, like picking his nose – yuck, and he'll never break your heart into a million pieces. It's a commitment-free way to indulge in the beautiful world of boy, because let's face it, boys are nice to look at.

Lola's crushin' on:
Johnny Depp – the world is most deffo a brighter shade of pink with Johnny in it.
Ian Watkins (lead singer of rock band Lost Prophets) – the ultimate rock boy – mmmmm.
Orlando Bloom – I think it would be rude and wrong NOT to be crushing on him.

Who are you currently crushing on?

....
....
....
....
....
....
....
....
....
....
....
....

Why does he make your heart melt?

....
....
....
....
....
....
....
....
....
....
....
....

Songs to fall in crush to...

When you're crazy in crush with that sweet-as-sugar boy type, melt your heart by listening to these...

Amy Winehouse – (There is) No Greater Love
Kylie – Can't Get You Out Of My Head
Olivia Newton John – Hopelessly Devoted To You
Joss Stone – Super Duper Love
Madonna – Crazy For You

Flirtability

If boy-ology was an 'A' Level subject, my best friend, Angel would score an 'A'. This is because she actually digs boys enough to want to step out with them. Angel is the queen of all things skirty-flirty and is the only one of us who has had a proper real life boyfriend for more than four weeks.

This makes her the official Think Pink skirty-flirty expert, a title well earned because she is able to attract a boy's attention with just one flutter of her super-mascara-ed lashes!

Being skirty-flirty isn't a bad thing, it's just a human instinct designed to let the boy-types know you're interested. So if you've ever smiled at a cute chico you didn't know, or made eye contact with a buff boy across the room – you were being skirty-flirty!

According to Angel, if you want your dream dude to know you're crushing on him, you're going to have to make it obvious. Most boys don't do complication, so you need to make sure the 'I-like-you' signals you're sending out are as strong as possible...

★ Think positive – if you think you haven't got a chance then that's the message you'll send out. Tell yourself you're sparkly-gorgeous (you really are, y'know) and you'll activate your skirty-flirty muscles.

★ Have fun – scientists in white coats have proved that people find it mucho hard to ignore happy people like yourself, so grab his attention by smiling and having fun.

★ Make contact – let him know you like him by making eye contact, holding his gaze and smiling right at him – he couldn't possibly resist!

★ Make your move – okay, so you've smiled, he's smiled back, he knows that you're fun to be around but there's a chance that he's just as worried about approaching you as you are him, so Think Pink and go to him – he'll be mucho chuffed!

★ Forget rejection – don't worry about whether he's going to say no, you'll never know unless you give it a go will you? So what if he does? At least you'll know the boy has no taste and you can move onto someone worthy of your attention.

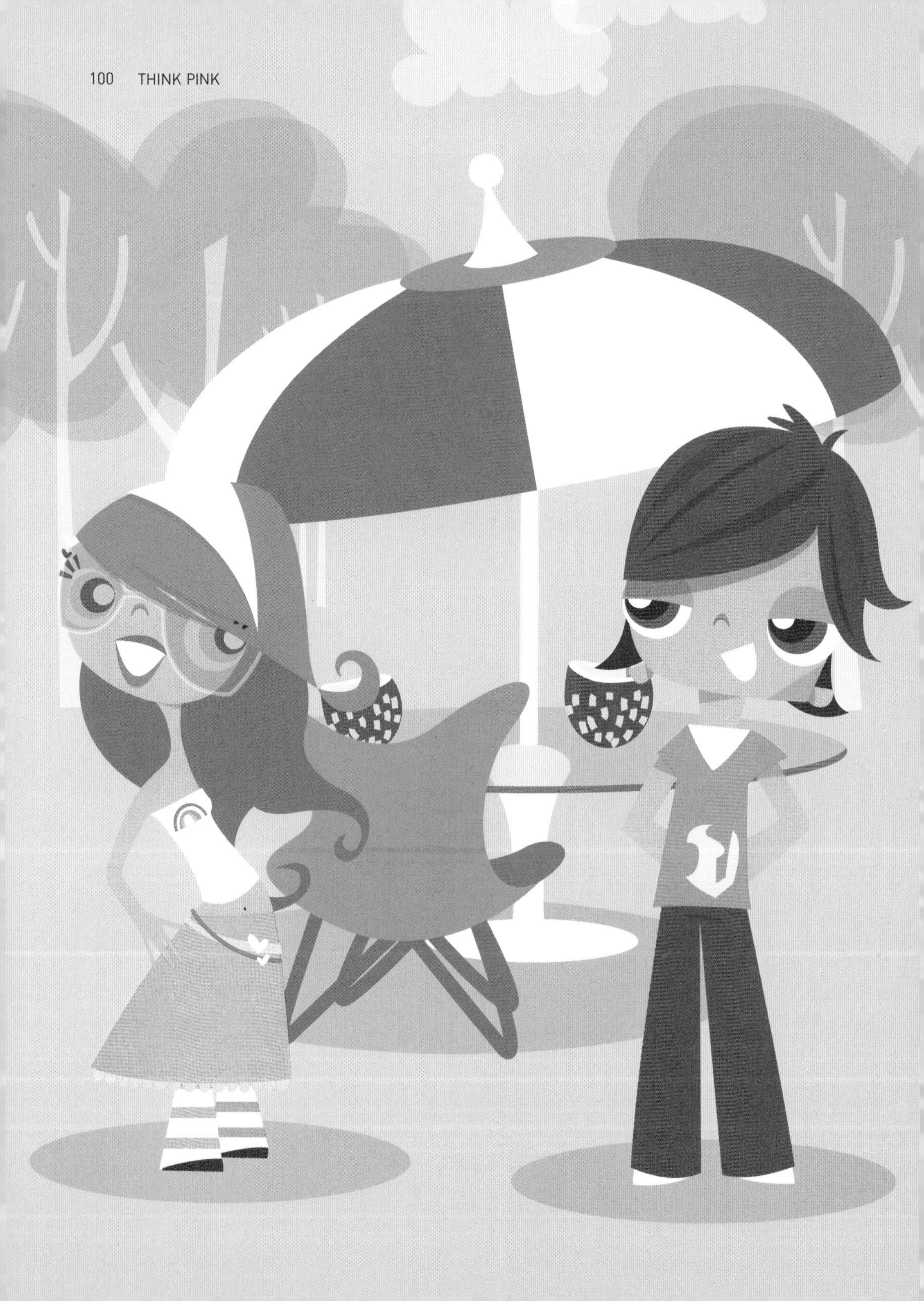

The deal on dating

Okay, so your boy crush has become a real life love interest who is swooning in your direction, which of course is all sorts of flattering, but before you commit to a date with your dream dude, Think Pink.

I thought sweet-as-sugar Jake would be the perfect date, in fact I'd run enough romantic scenarios in my head to know that a date with Jake would be more than great. So when he unexpectedly pulled me onto his lap at a party we were both at and put his hand on my knee in a really letchy not-nice-at-all kind of way, I realised that a date with Jake would actually be less than great. I couldn't think of anything worse.

Be yourself – don't try and be somebody you're not.

So before dating your dream dude, ask yourself if he is worthy of spending time with you because you are a princess after all, and as such, should be treated like one at all times. It would have been really easy for me to have thought 'wow, dream dude Jake is diggin' on me big time, I don't want to mess up my chances so I'll just go along with this' but by doing that I would have been being disrespectful to my sparkly-gorgeous self and that would have been all sorts of wrong.

Although I'm far too busy to fit a real life boy type into my schedule right now, for when I'm ready, I have a list of diggable qualities I will be looking for:
* ☆ Likes to laugh. Lots.
* ☆ An extensive knowledge of all things film related.
* ☆ Respects who I am and what I believe in, even if he doesn't always agree!
* ☆ Is not afraid to be himself, even if that means admitting he has every episode of The OC on tape.

✩ Makes me feel special – this can include anything from making me laugh, agreeing to watch an Audrey film, or mixing a CD of cool tunes just for me.

Unfortunately, Jake didn't possess any of these qualities. In fact, he didn't even come close. Now I'm not saying that every boy I'll ever date has to have every single quality, but knowing what I want and staying true to that is mucho important.

What qualities do you dig in a boy?

....
....
....
....
....
....
....
....
....
....
....
....
....
....
....
....
....
....
....
....
....
....
....
....
....
....
....
....
....
....
....

If you decide that a date with your dream dude is more than do-able just remember:

☆ Be yourself – don't try and be somebody you're not. You're feisty, fun fearless and fabulous – be proud of that!

☆ Don't change – he should be into the sparkle shine girl that is you so don't be tempted to say you love football just because he does. Chances are he might test your knowledge and then you'll be super stuck!

☆ Make sure you split your time fairly – a new beau can sometimes mean that schoolwork, friends and family end up taking a backseat. Friends will generally give you a period of time that is 'all about dream dude' the Pink Ladies suggest a month and then believe that normal friendship service should resume, but try to make it so that he doesn't become the centre of Pink World, just an exciting, cute new addition!

Avoid toxic boys

Bella doesn't dig boys. Bella positively spits blood at the mention of them. She likes guitars, and she likes girls who play guitars but she most deffo does not like boys. She did once, because she has kissed nine of them, which makes me think she liked them quite a lot. She is seventeen though, which means she's had much longer on the planet to work at the whole kissing boys thing, and much longer to discover that for every cool boy in the world there is a toxic boy too – this is why Bella doesn't like boys anymore. Y'see, toxic boys have made her bitter.

For those of you who haven't experienced a toxic boy, they're the kind of boy you wouldn't take home to your mum, not ever. They're the kind of boy who looks good on the outside but has a bad inside. He won't ring, he'll only bring you presents when he's done something wrong and he'll make you doubt how amazing you are. Boo.

My boy-crush Jake was a toxic boy, I just didn't know it at the time. So to make sure I only swoon at sweet-as-sugar cuties from now on, Bella has made me vow to avoid boys with toxic traits.

These are boys who:
☆   Don't listen – he thinks the world is all about him and is more than happy to spend an evening talking about himself.

☆ Aren't supportive – when you tell him you want to play lead guitar in a kick-ass girl band, he laughs. When you say you won't be able to see him tonight because you've got homework to do he gets in a huff.

☆ Get jealous – they stamp their feet and go red with rage when you spend time with your friends or talk to the guys from your English class.

☆ Say hurtful things to make you feel bad – remember, you rock and no bad-ass bully boy should tell you otherwise.

☆ Kiss other girls – wrong.

Toxic boys – don't call us...we'll call you. Actually, don't hold your breath, because we'll be stepping out with a chico who knows how fabulous we are.

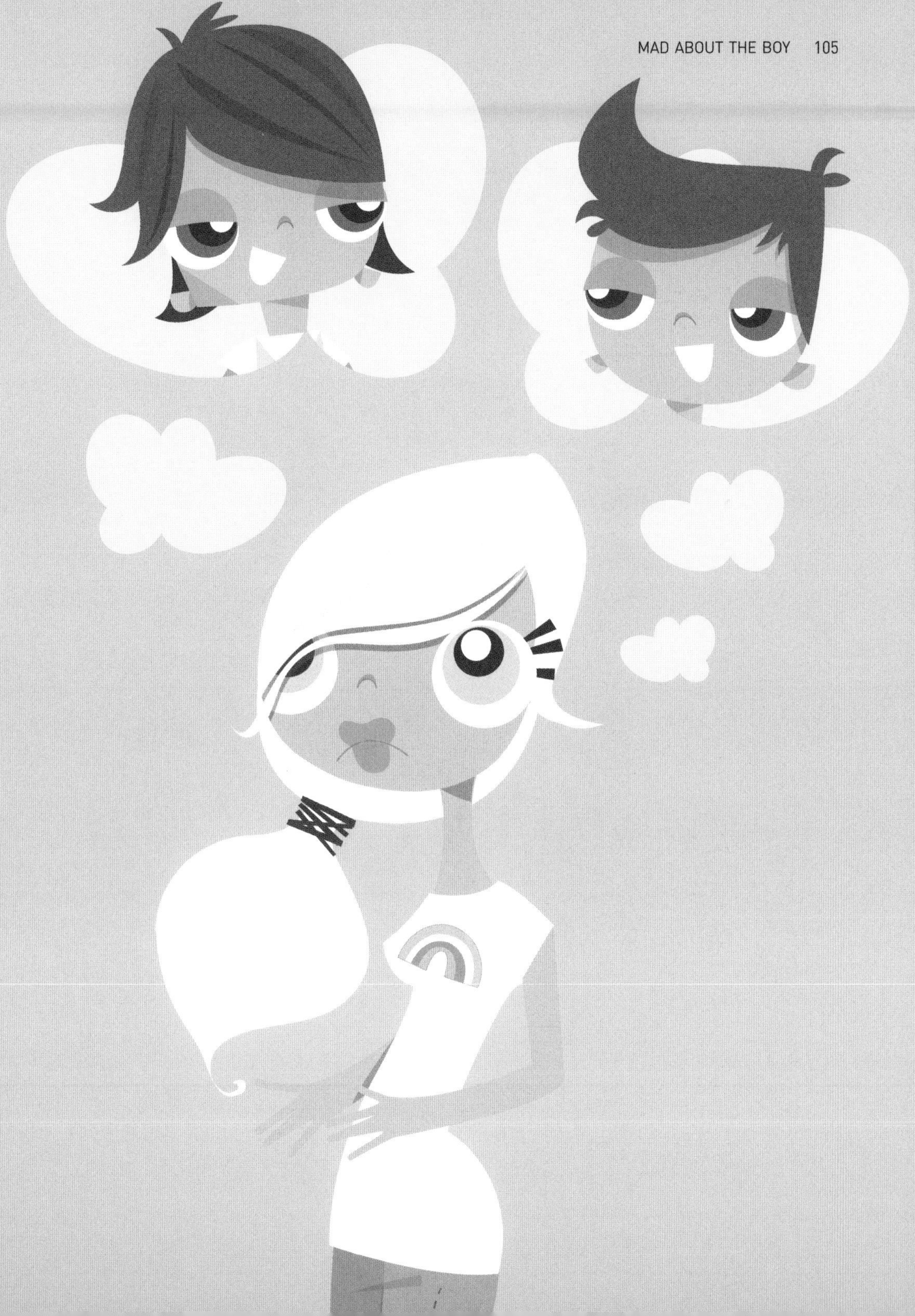

If Mister Right turns out to be Mister Wrong

Not every boy we date is going to be the dream dude we imagined, so it's pretty inevitable that at some point we're going to experience how sucky it is to be both the dumper and the dumpee. Boo.

If you're the dumper...

If you're not happy with your chico, you need to talk to him about it. Boy-types have feelings too and it's not fair to play with people's emotions, in the same way as it's not fair on yourself to stay with someone you no longer dig. Be truthful and honest and don't regret anything. Stand by your decision and don't dwell on what went wrong, just look on it as an experience that will assist you in finding your perfect partner.

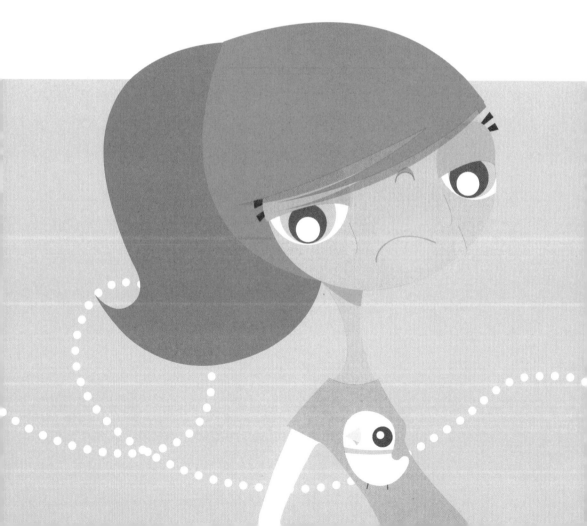

If you're the dumpee...

Grrrr. Unfortunately, there are boy-types in the world who can't see how fantastically fabulous you are and how lucky they are to be stepping out with you, but the trick here is to cry a lot and move on!

Your heart might feel like it's been smashed into a million pieces and that you'll never find anyone as cute as him to crush on EVER again...but you will, honest, and he'll be ten times better! Your friends will be there to support you but don't torture them by re-running the details of your break up eighty-four times. Talk to them about it, assess why you think it went wrong and then, to make sure you get everything out that hurts, write the rest in your diary.

Once you've used up a years supply of pink tissues, move on! How can you find a new chico to crush on if you're holding onto memories of your ex- boy?

Songs that will cause your mascara to run...
To make sure you get all the bad and sad stuff
out your system, put on these tunes and as JT
would say, 'cry me a river.' Sniff sniff...

Hole - Live Through This
Justin Timberlake – Cry Me a River
Maroon 5 – She Will be Loved
Dusty Springfield – All Cried Out
Anything by Radiohead

The boy mate

Not only is Angel the queen of all things skirty-flirty but she also has that rare yummy treat - a boy mate. He's called Charlie and he is ice cream covered in chocolate sprinkles. They go shopping together and sometimes even go to the cinema – but they never kiss, even though we think they should.

But Angel disagrees.

She says that a platonic boy friend like Charlie is for life not just for smooches and she wouldn't want to ruin their friendship by ever locking lips. Cute.

Boy mates are great because:
* ☆ They are boy shaped yet don't give you a messy head
* ☆ They are extremely low maintenance
* ☆ He'll offer great advice on what boys really think

It's cool to be single

Don't panic if you're not into those boy types or if life is so busy you just haven't got time to fit them in because I'm proof that being single rocks! I like boys a lot, but I love doing my own girl thing more. I fill my life with fun things and make myself happy by doing the things I love. It also means I can get on with my school work without distraction, pamper myself on a regular basis and spend time working on project FUTURE (you'll find out more about that later). But most importantly, life is so much less stressy when it is boy-drama free and that is most deffo a good thing.

What do you love about being a single girl?

....
....
....
....
....
....
....
....
....
....
....
....
....
....
....
....
....
....
....
....
....
....
....
....
....
....

My declaration of independence

In celebration of being young, free and single I will:

★ Treat myself to something special at least once a week – I'm worth it!

★ Wear blue eye shadow

★ Tie my hair back with a pair of pink fishnets and wear my pyjamas all **weekend – bliss!**

★ Put on my favourite CD and sing along karaoke style

★ Crush on boys if I feel like it, because some are very nice to look at

Your turn...

In celebration of being young free and single I will:

....

....

....

....

....

....

....

....

....

....

....

....

....

....

....

....

....

....

....

....

....

....

....

....

....

....

....

Don't worry, be happy

'...FILL YOUR LIFE WITH SUNSHINE-FILLED, CANDY-KISSED MOMENTS...'

Being too busy to breathe means you miss out on all the amazing moments that your life is filled with on a daily basis.

Is your Hello Kitty organiser so packed with 'things-to-do' that you feel positively worn out just looking at it? Do you put yourself under pressure to perform well in exams? Are you too busy worrying about what other people think of you to treat yourself like the princess you undoubtedly are?

If you answered 'yes' to any of these questions, you are on a helter skelter ride that leads to a stressy, messy head and belly-knots.

This is not good.

Being too busy to breathe means you miss out on all the amazing moments that your life is filled with on a daily basis. That cheeky wink from the football captain or the compliment you received about your new sparkly-gorgeous killer heels are pushed aside because you're too busy stressing about homework or the fight you had with your parentals.

You see chica, it's all about perspective.

You could spend your whole life getting all sweaty and unnecessary about anything and everything but this will ultimately just zap your energy, leaving you no time to sunbathe in the sunshine-filled, candy-kissed moments of the here and now, and that would just be all sorts of wrong.

So, to banish that messy, stressy head upon arrival and achieve instant calm...Think Pink!

cheeky wink from
the football captain

How stressy are you?

Are you a moody 'mare or a laid back lass?

You're stuck in a traffic jam on the hottest day of the year, a boy in the car next to yours sticks out his tongue, do you:
a. Wind down the window and tell him to grow up.
b. Laugh at him.

You've just put on your new to-die-for top when your bro squirts tomato sauce down the front, do you
a. Scream and shout claiming you want a new family.
b. Grab a cloth – quick.

Your friend has just got back from her hols and she won't stop talking about this 'amazing' new friend she made, do you:
a. Tell her she has to choose between her old and new friends.
b. Tell her the other girl sounds amazing and that you would love to meet her.

You're finding it difficult to walk in your new sequinned spangly boots and accidently trip over in front of a v.cute, tastycake, do you:

a. Scream at him to stop gawping.

b. Laugh – what else can you do?

You're in need of a quick cash injection from your pa, do you:

a. Stamp your foot and refuse to move from in front of the TV screen until he gives in

b. Offer to make him a cup of coffee if he agrees to lend you a fiver

Mostly a's...

Oh my stars, you're boiling babe! You fly off the handle at the smallest of things and won't let friends or family forget when they've upset you. Before lashing out, take deep breaths and think before you speak because all that pent-up anger will lead to a messy head and you saying stuff you don't mean.

Mostly b's...

You're cool chica! You're super calm and know that life is all about chillin', not shouting. When temperatures soar and tempers fray you choose not to let things get you down, 'coz let's face it, life's too short to sweat about the small stuff, right?

Trigger happy

...pull the happiness trigger at any given moment.

I'm one of those girls who used to be so caught up in what might happen that, when I got a 'C' for my essay, I thought I might not get into college and then I'd never be able to go to university, so I'd never get my dream job which meant...Aaaaaggghhh, STOP! My imagination would always be two steps ahead making up a less than happy ending to any scenario I'd happened to find myself in.

Fed up of living my life in a badly scripted film, I became a 'Trigger-happy-Tina' – she's the girl who knows what puts a smile on her bee-stung, ruby lips so that when life gets that little bit too real-lifey and stressy situations threaten to knock her off her pink round-toed mules she's armed and ready to pull the happiness trigger at any given moment.

For example, before I knew Jake was a letchy jock boy, I was mortified to find out he was stepping out with the evil Eva Satine. It was a heart-breaking, anger inducing situation that I had no control over, so I had two options...

1. To get super mad and cry. A lot. This would make me feel good for, ooh, five minutes, but all I'd be left with is a sore foot from the pavement stomping and a broken heart...

or

2. To Think Pink instead of seeing red and feel sorry for Jake as he would have to endure the company of Eva. There was no denying that the girl could throw an outfit together, but with her undoubtable style and 'just-stepped-out-of-a-salon' hair came the most horrible of insides. So if Jake wanted to reside in a world that was all-about-Eva, then cool, he'd just be missing out on the feisty, fun, fearless and fabulous ME! Yes, at the time it felt like my heart had been ripped out and stamped on, but I had a finger on my happiness trigger and I knew that the ultimate candy-kissed way to put a smile back on my lip-glossed lips was to watch my entire collection of limited edition Audrey Hepburn DVDs in my comfy pyjamas and pink, fluffy slippers...

How to...become a 'Trigger-happy-Tina'

You need to have a hefty stock of happiness ammunition so begin by making a list of all the things that are guaranteed to make you smile from ear to ear, and could quite possibly make it last all year:

....

....

....

....

....

....

....

....

....

....

....

....

....

....

....

....

....

....

....

....

....

....

....

....

Things that make me jump-in-the-air happy are: Strawberry flavoured Angel Delight, the Audrey Hepburn DVD collection, splashing in puddles, painting my toe nails with 'Brighton Rock' pink polish, kingsize chocolate bars, the seaside, window shopping, swinging on a swing and my stupidly huge pink, fluffy slippers... Now the trick is, when that hefty black cloud threatens to rain on your pink parade, whether it's an argument, a bad mark for your essay or someone's being a Negative Nina, pull your happiness trigger and fill your life to the brim with your very own cherry-picked cheery times!

Happy Days

There is nothing more satisfying than waking up, rubbing last night's smudged mascara from my eyes and realising it's the weekend. Being Saturday happy is my absolute favourite kind of happy, because it's all about the joie de vivre. It's about no school, wearing dangly earrings without the risk of confiscation, smiling lots, skipping instead of walking, hanging with my crew, candyfloss kisses and laughing out loud – I declare everyday a Saturday!

What would be the perfect way to spend a Saturday?

....
....
....
....
....
....
....
....
....
....
....
....
....
....
....
....
....
....
....
....
....
....
....
....
....

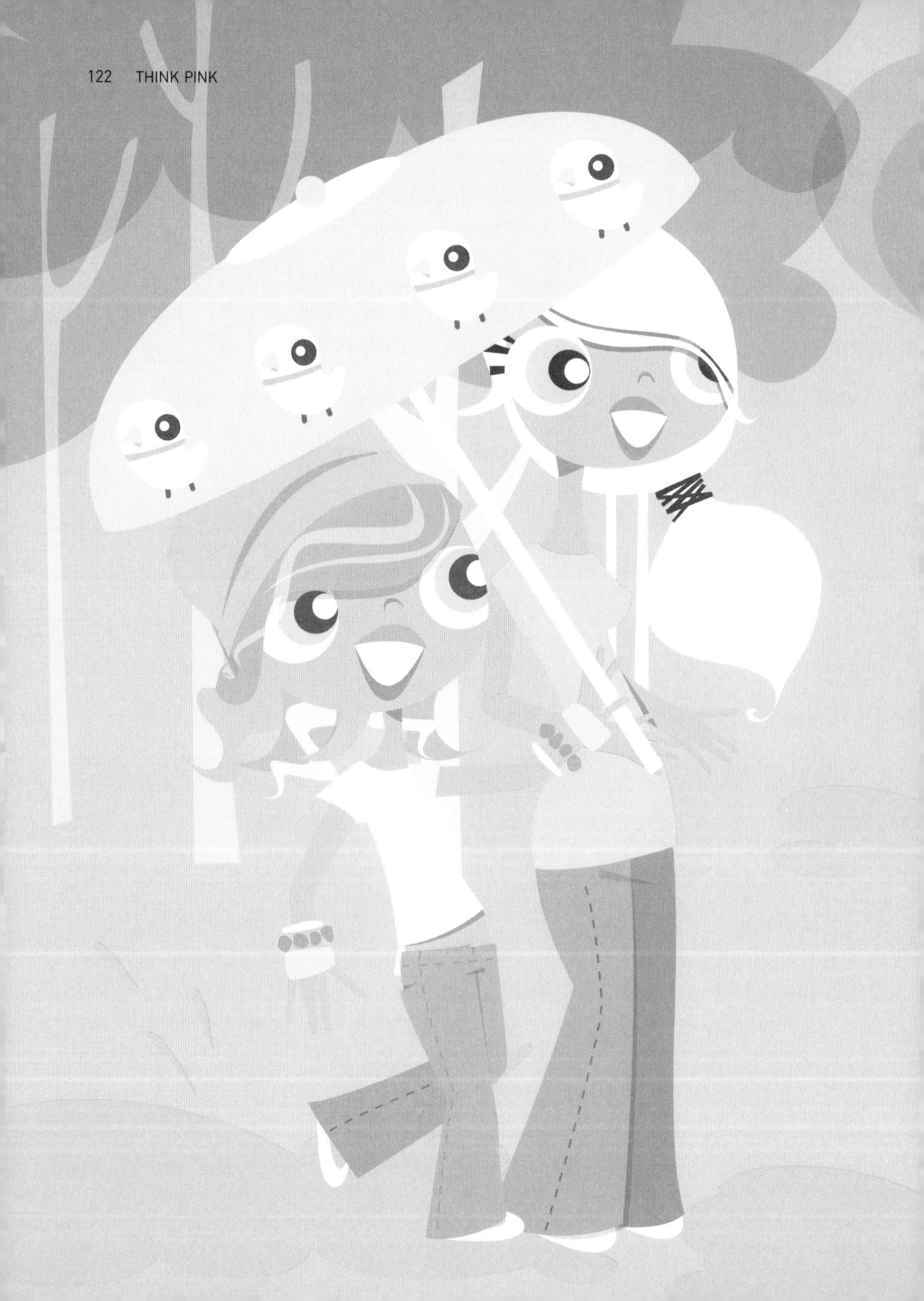

splashing in puddles

Smile!

The most important item you are going to find in my Think Pink vanity case is... a smile.

Don't laugh, a smile is by far the coolest accessory I own, unlike my very gorgeous, but slightly tarnished diamante bracelet, it goes with absolutely everything I own. People are more attracted to me when I wear it and it can instantly change the way I look and feel, try it out. Stand in front of the mirror without smiling. Now put a smile on your gorgeous face and see how it changes your whole physical appearance. Your eyes will sparkle and you will instantly feel mucho better just by turning that frown upside down.

Make it part of your new routine to smile at everyone you meet and if someone hasn't got a smile give them yours!

Giggle kit

As well as smiling, the pink ladies love to giggle, we do it all the time. Even when we're not supposed to, in fact it's best when you're not supposed to. Laughter and smiles are infectious and they are a great way of releasing tension or negative thoughts so put together your own giggle kit for whenever you need a quick boost of giggles. Any time you're feeling a bit tense, pick your favourite giggle maker and banish the badness!

Lola's giggle kit:
A selection of funny DVDs
Someone relentlessly tickling me
Going to the zoo – those monkeys with the l'il pink bums can never fail to make me laugh, not never!

What would you put in your giggle kit?

....

....

....

....

....

....

....

....

....

....

....

....

....

....

....

....

....

....

....

Let's get physical!

Exercise is a pretty new edition to Pink World. Don't get me wrong, I've always known that it existed, it's just that, until now, I've chosen to ignore anything that involved sweating in favour of a substantial amount of napping under my much-loved, tea-stained duvet. But Angel had other ideas.

She had read an article in one of her many glossy magazines about how exercise was the key to banishing stress and making us happy, she was convinced that if we didn't exercise, we would become stressy, and stress would means wrinkles. I tried to point out that she was only fourteen and that wrinkles were probably not a cause for concern just yet, but there was something about the way she handed me the neon pink trainers and legwarmer combo that suggested they weren't just a 70's retro fashion statement, she meant business.

Our initiation to the world of physical activity was a two-hour DVD of grapevines and star jumps with two buff beauties and a reality TV star. We got incredibly red-faced and slightly sweaty in the process, but the magazine article was right, my, those journo types are so wise, because by the time we had finished, my worries had vanished and we were both high on a happy vibe! So much so, that we didn't even eat the chocolate bar we had been saving to congratulate ourselves for completing exercise!

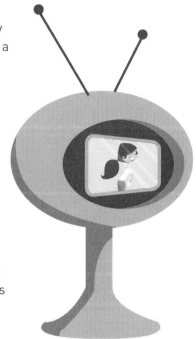

Angel and I are now of the understanding that exercise is the ultimate in stress relief because when you feel good physically, you feel good emotionally, fact. You don't have to be a fitness freak to feel the benefit of exercise, just thirty minutes, five times a week, will make the hugest difference. It will boost your energy levels and release a whole load of endorphins, your body's happy hormone, to make you feel sparkly-gorgeous and stress free.

How cool is that?

doin' the
grapevine

Rock your body

If just the thought of having to wear a tracksuit is causing you to break out in a sweat, don't worry because exercise isn't all about fitness classes and competitive sport - who knew? There are plenty of fun and fabulous ways to keep our bodies movin' and endorphins pumpin' try these for size:

★ Be a Roller Girl and invest in a pair of 70's retro roller boots. Forget blading, if you want to look hot-to-trot while partaking in physical exercise then roller-skating is most definitely the way to go. Gold spangled hot pants are optional.

★ These boots are made for walking, and that's just what they'll do...Going for a walk is not only a fab way to keep fit but it also gives you a chance to dream, people watch and see things you never normally see when you're on the bus.

★ Fly a kite. You have to climb to the top of a very high hill before you can begin, you have to then run down the aforementioned hill to get the kite in the air, and then you will have to scale a tall tree when it inevitably gets caught in the branches.

★ Throwing a Frisbee. All you need is your Pink Ladies, a park and a good Frisbee-throwing arm. Unfortunately, I have difficulty catching a cold, so it's not a game I'm incredibly good at, but the fun potential is huge and normally comes in the form of laughter, at my expense!

★ Shake your booty and crown yourself the Dancing Queen. There is nothing better in this world than putting on a great tune and dancing as if no one is watching. Shut the bedroom door, put on a booty-shaking disco classic, my favourites are 'Yes Sir, I Can Boogie' by Baccara or 'Rock the Boat' by Hues Corporation and then girlfriend, shake it, shake it, shake it like a Polaroid picture!

flying my kite

"

Before seeing the world through pink–tinted glasses, my world was a boring shade of grey and that affected how I felt about myself and the people around me.

"

Colour me happy!

Before seeing the world through pink–tinted glasses, my world was a boring shade of grey and that affected how I felt about myself and the people around me. You see, colour can enhance your mood and even change how you feel about yourself physically, certain colours make us feel happy while others give us confidence.

Pink World is so cool because pink is the colour of candyfloss and everything prettilicious. It's the universal colour of love and, if you love pink, it means you respect and accept yourself for who you are: you're a great friend who loves to give hugs and affection and you're really approachable.

Check out what your favourite shade reveals about you and the effect that it can have on your mood...

Red: You're full of self-confidence and an inspiration to everyone. You're honest and an action girl who really makes things happen. Wearing red will not only recharge your batteries when you're feeling tired, but it will also make sure you get noticed.

Orange: You're an outgoing party girl who tends to have a constant smile on her face, you're always first to suggest a party! If you're lacking in confidence or feeling a bit depressed splash on some orange accessories – you glow girl!

Yellow: You're super-intelligent with so much to give – expect amazing things from the girl in yellow! Yellow is a great sunny shade to cheer you up when you're feeling a bit grumpy.

Green: Although green is the colour of jealousy and envy, if you love green it means you're a relaxed kinda girl who doesn't take life too seriously. Green is a very romantic colour – who knew? So wear this to attract the attention of a crush.

Blue: Down to earth, fair and honest, you're known for your loyalty. You hate to fall out with your friends and will do anything to keep the peace. Wear blue when you want the people around you to chill out and avoid arguments.

Indigo: You are super-deep and very creative, your mates rely on you in times of difficulty. Indigo is soothing and means that it is a fab colour for helping you to relax – ahhh feel the chill!

Violet: You know where you're going in life and your mates look up to you and respect you, yet you're too modest to even realise! Violet is a great colour for taking into exams as it keeps you alert and focused.

Lola Lovin' Time

'...I WANT TO BE ALONE...'

Now, I know it's not all about me, but Lola Lovin' time is something I do on a regular basis.

It's simple really, I'm my favourite person in the world, so it makes sense that I want to spend time hanging out with myself doing the things I love to do. It means I can put toothpaste on my spots, soak in the bath until I resemble a wrinkly prune, go to the beach with my notebook, watch 'Moulin Rouge' and cry at the same bit every time or jump up and down on my bed ala Billy Elliot in my pink-trimmed Paul Frank knickers and vest combo, just because...well...just because I can!

Plan your perfect 'me time' session here...What would you do?
Where would you do it?

Chill your boots, chica!

Chillin' really isn't that difficult once you get the hang of it, in fact I'm practically professional at it now! Here are some fun and fabulous ways to chill your boots and appreciate the company of that amazing, star-shine sparkle girl...YOU!

★ Ask the parentals if you can book the bathroom for the night and spend the entire evening pampering yourself silly. Fill the bath with a relaxing bubble foam, put a mud pack on that gorgeous face and just lie back and relax!

★ If it's a crazy, hazy sunny summer day, have an adventure! You may not be able to afford to go further than your back garden but all you need is a notebook and a head full of dreams to realise that there are no limitations to where your imagination can take you!

★ Flick the 'off' switch in that hectic head and admire and adore the stars of the silver screen. If you don't fancy going solo to the cinema, then make sure you've got full control of the DVD player and immerse yourself in another world...

★ Make your bedroom your personal sanctuary, a place for dreams and thoughts and ideas to happen. Set the scene by dimming the lights, burning some candles and putting on some turn-your-mood-around tunes. Now make yourself comfy, close your eyes and take yourself on a daydream holiday...Go wherever you want to go, do all the things you've always wanted to do. Now focus on why these things and places are important to you and, as you do, relax your body starting with your tootsies... ahh, bliss!

★ Paint a picture, read a book (I recommend Stargirl by Jerri Spinelli, Gingerbread by Rachel Cohn, The Misfits by James Howse) splash in a huge puddle in just your flip-flops, get crafty because stichin' is no longer the hobby of grannies or colour a picture in your lil' sister's colouring book and don't worry about keeping in the lines – there doesn't always have to be an end result, just have fun enjoying the moment!

How do you chill out chica?

chillin' in the garden

Dare to Dream

'REACH FOR THE STARS...'

TIFFANY & CO

113

NYPD

My wish list for the future is huge and ever-changing. In fact, I add to it weekly. This isn't because I'm a girl, although changing our mind is what we girls do best, it isn't because I'm a Gemini either, even though Geminis are renown for being indecisive and fickle, no, it's because I Think Pink.

Living in a world where people knock success and demand that we constantly define ourselves can make having a dream a bit tricky. But when you Think Pink, it just means there are endless possibilities and the only limit is your imagination – the future is most deffo pink!

What's your destiny direction?

Your personality can give you some neon-coloured clues to your glitter-filled destiny, what does the future have in store for you?

In class you're working on a group project, you're the one:
a. Making a to-do list and setting deadlines
b. Planning how to make this presentation look as fabulous as possible

When asked to describe you, your friends say:
a. She's a control freak!
b. She's totally out there!

Phew! You've just handed a big school project in, you're thinking:
a. 'Have I done it the 'right' way?' Chica, you're such a perfectionist!
b. 'What am I doing tonight?' - You're a busy girl who has not time to sweat the small stuff

Your bedroom is:
a. Totally tidy - well how else would you know where everything is?
b. A complete mess - why waste time tidying when you could be doing something much more fun instead?

It's Saturday morning and your alarm has gone off at 6am, do you:
a. Get up, why else would you set an alarm?
b. Throw a pillow at it and turn over

Mostly a's:

You love taking charge and are most happiest when people depend on you as it makes you feel all responsible and useful. You need a routine and would thrive doing something that has a set schedule where you are in control.

Mostly b's:

You're naturally upbeat and your imagination is filled-to-the-brim with big ideas that just need to get out. You're a dreamer and believe that anything is possible, in fact, this will most deffo be the key to your success.

Project FUTURE

Whether you know exactly what you want out of life (you lucky chica, you!) or you're like me, and are still undecided, Project FUTURE is the most amazing way to make sure that your future is the brightest shade of pink! Devised by the Pink Ladies, and myself natch, Project FUTURE is everything a boring-snoring session with a career guidance type isn't.

In fact, I promise you, this is one project you will actually want to work on! But in order for Project FUTURE to be a huge success, there is one important requirement, yep, you've guessed it, you've got to Think Pink!

Project FUTURE files:
A great way to create a glitter-filled vision of your future in front of your very eyes is to unleash the art girl in you and make a kick-ass Project FUTURE file! (Mine's pink with guitar boys, silver screen goddesses and cheesy song lyrics written on it – how are you going to decorate yours?)

The idea is to make a journal or scrapbook and fill it with your dreams, thoughts, newspaper clippings, pictures and quotes that will all help you to make a hot date with your destiny.

So next time you're flipping through a magazine and you see a picture of a city you'd like to visit, rip it out and stick it in your Project FUTURE file, or maybe you're reading an article about someone doing a job that you might be interested in doing – rip it out and stick it in your Project FUTURE file, or maybe...you get the picture, right?

Detect your destiny

Some people are super lucky and know what they want to do from a really young age, while others, like myself, are still undecided. I still don't have a really clear idea of what I actually want to do in the world yet (c'mon, I am still only fourteen!), but I do know what I love and what I'm good at, which is a pretty good place to start I reckon!

What you're passionate about can be a signpost to destination FUTURE so, detective girl, dust for fingerprints and search for clues marked 'destiny'! Pink super-sleuth costume and ridiculously big magnifying glass are, of course, optional.

What's your passion? Forget crushing on boy types, I'm talking real heart-squeezing passion that makes you feel like you want to do what you're doing forever.

....
....
....
....
....
....
....
....
....
....
....
....
....
....

What do you dig doing?

....
....
....
....
....
....
....
....

....
....

What are your unique talents?

....
....
....
....
....
....
....
....
....
....
....
....

What achievements are you most proud of in your life so far?

....
....
....
....
....
....
....
....
....
....
....
....
....
....
....

Now get to work lil' miss Sherlock, and take a close look, are there any patterns? What gets you goosebumpy with excitement when you think about it? Keep that excitement, hold it in a really tight bear hug and use it as the fuel you're going to need to dream big!

Daydream believer

> Daydreaming is the chance to think big, make plans and ponder the endless possibilities that life has in store.

I have always been accused of being queen daydreamer. Instead of taking this as the criticism it was intended to be, I accepted the title with pleasure. Not only because it meant another sparkly-gorgeous trinket to add to my collection, but also because... well, what can I say? Daydreaming is cool.

Daydreaming is the chance to think big, make plans and ponder the endless possibilities that life has in store. In fact, your school even sets aside a whole 45 minutes dedicated to the pure, unadulterated pleasure that is daydreaming, it's called Maths class – use it wisely chica!

Seriously, by daring to dream you open your life up to a world of sugar-coated, amazing experiences. Without dreams Martin Luther King would not have rocked our world by being the greatest human rights activist who ever lived Oprah Winfrey, one of my favourite leading ladies, would not be the influential queen of all things media that she is today and Marilyn Monroe would not have become the ultimate silver screen legend that she undoubtedly was, so what are you waiting for?

Start dreaming...NOW!

Daydream kit
You will need:
An open mind
Creative imagination

Instructions:
Put aside any obstacles - family
responsibilities, lack of money, where
you're from, what people might think
and sit back and relax, letting your mind
explore the endless possibilities for
your gorgeous, glitter-filled life!

Write foot forward

All the time your dreams stay in your head, they'll remain just that, dreams. So instead of storing them away until your next daydreaming day, create a dream map. Stick a photo or better still, draw a picture of yourself in the centre of a plain piece of paper. Around you put all the things you're passionate about that fuelled your dreams, then, now here comes the fun bit, write down all your dreams, everything from being a political activist to owning a Prada purse - make it as bold and as colourful as you want, this is your future baby!

By writing down your dreams and putting copies of them in places that you'll look every day, like your memo board, your journal or your schoolbag, they will soon become your most important 'to-do' list of all, your Project FUTURE to-do list!

My passions are: watching films, travelling, reading books, fashion, glamour, customising clothes, making a difference.

In my super-sun-splashed life I would like to: be in a band, help to beat poverty, edit my own magazine, make a difference, write and direct a kick-ass movie, visit New York, design my own clothing range, write a book, earn enough money to open a vintage clothing store, become an art girl illustrator, write poetry, live in a house with pink décor.

Now fill in your dream map opposite following the instructions here:

Example of my dream map

travelling

edit my own magazine

glamour

visit New York

= What I would like to do

= My Passions

put your
picture here

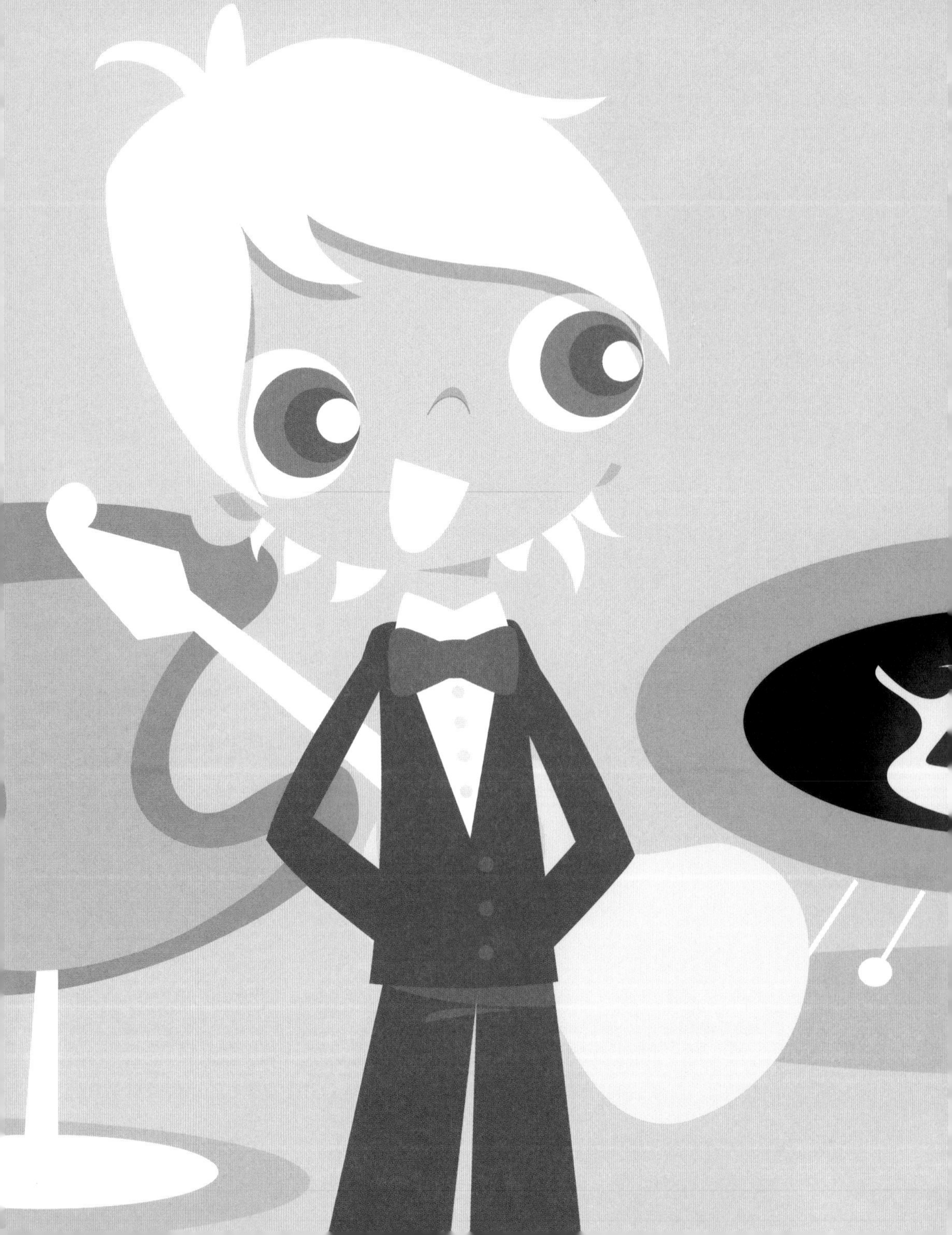

my dream house!

Take a bite

Once you've seen the possibilities for project FUTURE, you've then got to work on believing it can happen, because seeing is believing, sista! If you've got the ability to dream something in your head, whether it's running a marathon or singing on stage then there is absolutely no reason why you can't make it a reality.

As you're already aware, when you Think Pink, just about anything can be compared to chocolate and your dreams are no exception. Take my dream to 'make a difference.' Currently, it seems the most monumentally huge, sick-inducing bar of chocolate I have seen in my entire life I really want to eat it but I just don't know where to begin.

If you've got the ability to dream something in your head...
then there is absolutely no reason why you can't make it a reality.

Luckily, I'm not the type to be deterred from eating yummy chocolate, so instead of trying to tackle the mammoth bar in one go, I've broken the bar into manageable bite-size chunks, I asked myself what exactly could I do to make a difference, and then made a list...

- ✰ I could volunteer at the local charity shop
- ✰ I could organise a book collection for children in Africa
- ✰ I could buy a wrist band to show my support towards beating world poverty

I now have three achievable goals that will put me well on my way to making a difference. Having goals and achieving them is an important part of having a glitter-filled purposeful life, so reach for the stars chica, just make sure you reach for the nearest one first!

Write your dream wish list:

....
....
....
....
....
....
....
....
....
....
....
....
....
....
....
....
....
....
....
....
....
....
....
....
....
....
....
....
....
....
....
....
....
....
....
....

Choose one wish.

What goals could you set to make it a reality?

....

....

....

....

....

....

....

....

....

....

....

....

....

....

....

....

....

....

....

....

....

....

....

....

....

....

....

....

....

....

....

....

....

....

....

....

Be prepared

Achieving your dreams is only an unclimbable mountain if you're not prepared for the journey. If you set out to climb it in a pair of killer-heels and a vest top with only a chocolate bar for sustenance, chances are you're only going to get as far as the car park, right?

But if you do your research and plan a route you'll be more than equipped for the journey ahead.

Be prepared...if something interests you, find out more about it.

'Be prepared' isn't just a motto for those dudes in cute shorts who tie knots, it's your one-way ticket to success. Think about when you dig a celeb-type, if you're anything like me, you'll go completely out of your way to access every bit of information you possibly can about them. The same should apply to a place you'd like to visit or a job you'd like to do - if something interests you, find out more about it.

When I was younger, I wanted to become a doctor. That was until I found out you'd have to study for seven whole years, not be scared of blood, be able to pronounce long words and know what they mean! Now for some, this would encourage them to open a bank account and start saving for university, but for me, the idea of studying for seven years before I got to use a stethoscope sounded just a teeny bit too long, so I crossed it off my list.

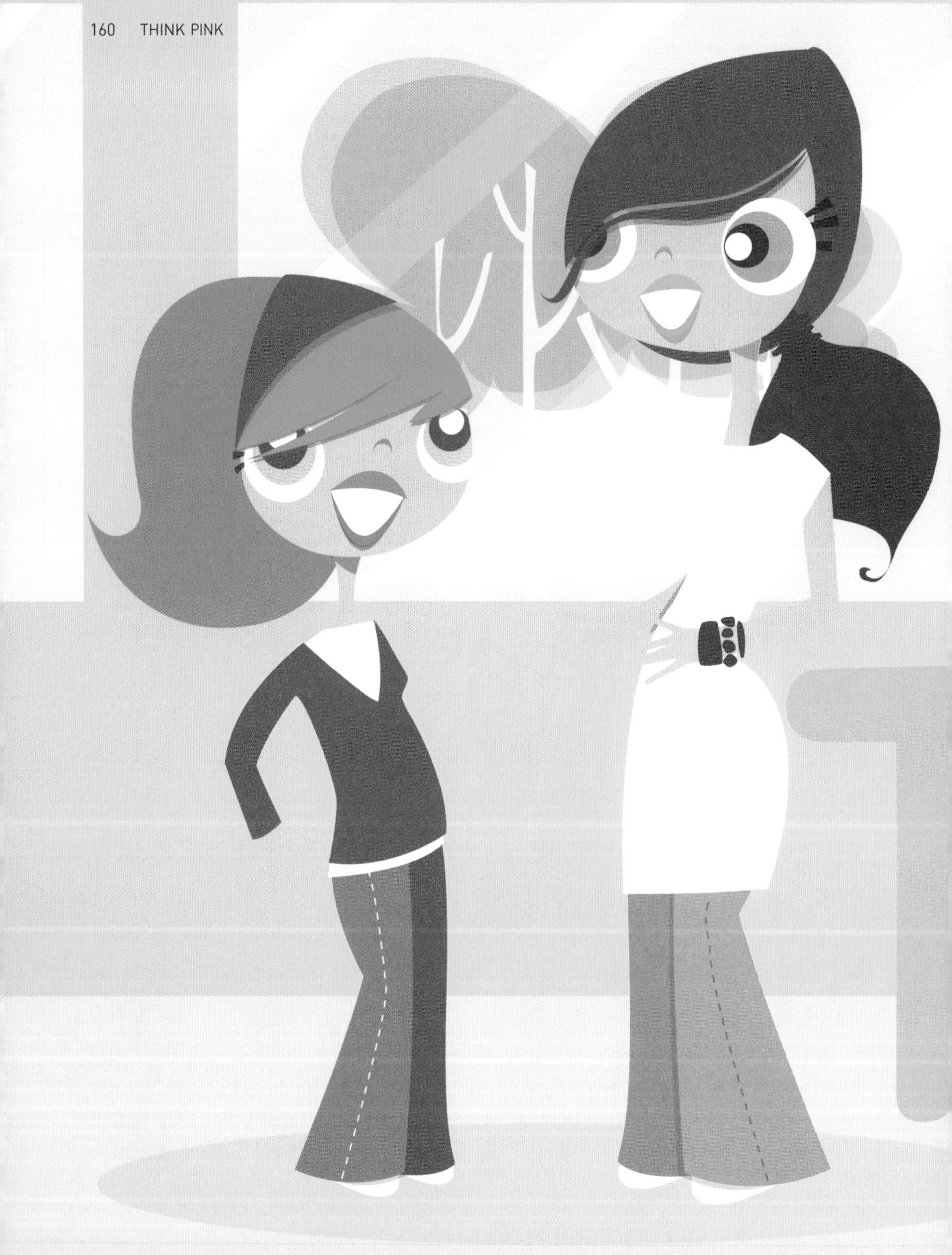

To make sure you dig what you do:

✦ Research – go to the library or log on to the internet and find out more about the things that interest you, that way you have the information you need to make informed choices about your star-shaped future.

✦ Read – autobiographies of peoples' lives are cool, there's absolutely hundreds to choose from out there and not only do you get to be super nosey, you get an insight into what life is really like as a film star, gardener, doctor etc... My personal favourites include: DV by Diana Vreeland – she was the sassy editor of Vogue, j'adore her and this book mostest. Absolutely Now! by Lynne Frank – it's said that Lynne was the lady that the character Eddie in 'Absolutely Fabulous' was based on! Business as Unusual by Anita Roddick – The woman behind The Body Shop had a huge vision, find out how she made it a reality.

✦ Work experience – there's no better way to decide if you're going to like something than to try it first hand.

✦ Network – ask your family or friends if they know of anyone who has the kind of jobs you're interested in and find out what it's really like, good and bad.

I need a hero

When planning for your amazing future, you don't have to do it alone, you know. I've got a list of leading ladies who between them offer me the inside scoop on what it's really like to do certain jobs, live in certain countries and to be successful – they're my mentors and they rock!

A mentor is somebody who will help you achieve your goals, my leading ladies all offer their advice and perspective to help make my path to my dream destiny that little bit less bumpy:

Bella - she's helping me to play guitar as if my life depended on it.
Audrey Hepburn - she rocked in every outfit she ever wore, she had the greatest vocab and she'd steal the screen in every scene – she demanded attention and, oh my stars, did she get it! She has encouraged me to do the same.
Gwen Stefani - she's kooky and honest, qualities I admire and strive for.
Art girl - Andrea - she's a film student at the local college who is currently making a film about 'teen queens' and has asked me to star in it! I agreed on the basis that she filled me in on her experiences studying film so far.
Aunt Tallullah – she's a cool fashion queen living in New York and she sends me postcards of the Empire State building with cute stories about her life in the city of my dreams – I stick them all in my Project FUTURE file to remind me how much I really want to go there!

A mentor is somebody who will help you achieve your goals

A role model may be a celeb, someone you've read about or someone you know, basically it can be anyone who has kick-ass qualities that you admire, provides you with a different perspective of the world and inspires you to live your life unlimited!

Who are your role models?

....
....
....
....
....
....
....
....
....
....
....
....
....

What qualities do you admire about them?

....
....
....
....
....
....
....
....
....
....
....
....
....
....
....
....
....

It's cool to admire people and ask for help but don't try to be them or walk in their shoes. Learn from them and be inspired but remember, you are your own star-shaped hero and you can make your own mule-shaped footprints!

This girl will rock your world...

While surfing the net for my Project FUTURE file I found Amy Davis. She's an illustrator girl who can make beautiful things happen when she puts pen to paper. She is also capable of changing your life. Fact.

If you haven't got a role model, try Amy for size. I defy you not to be blown away!
She says: In five words I am...Goofy, Loud, Fun, Glam, Chatty

YOU ARE ALL STARS!

As a teen girl, life was... HELL! I grew up in Long Island, New York and, baby, that sucked. It was the land of SUBURBIA and lotsa mean, lame horrible types...myself included. I was so self-hatin' and insecure and pimply and had a BAD PERM. I JUDGED EVERYONE AND EVERYTHING! Until I realised it's just l'il old me that was the thing that made me so mean and sick!

How I became an illo-girl... I went to art school and that totally was NOT for me. It tripped me up for seven years after. My career started when my hubbie sent PAPER mag a doodle I did. They called me up, flew me to NYC, and had me draw that season's fashion collections then they GAVE me the COVER and a 17 page spread! WOAH!! Total Cinderella stuff...

My tips for success are... LIKE ATTRACTS LIKE put out goodness and, baby, that's what you'll get! I'm inspired by... EVERYTHING. Life and the stars inside each person inspire moi...YOU ARE ALL STARS!

Check out her site: **www.amydavis.com**

Take action!

Life rewards action. Fact.

Success isn't just for the select few y'know, it's for those who are willing to put in the time and effort required to make it happen. On a purely superficial note, and with an extremely tenuous link to project FUTURE, allow me to demonstrate how you can make what might seem virtually impossible completely do-able by taking action!

When shopping with Angel recently, I fell head over scuffed-up trainers in love with a pair of pastel pink, ballerina pumps in a shop window. I saw myself wearing them with my retro style pastel pink prom dress and I knew instantly that they would complement each other like a super-size dish of strawberries and cream. I wanted them. A lot.

But unfortunately I had no money. Boo.

I was left with two choices:

1. Resign myself to the fact that I would never own such beautiful footwear and that my feet were destined to live their life in a pair of Dunlop Green Flash...

OR

2. Find a way that does not involve robbing a bank (the black horizontal stripes that robbers wear is so unflattering) to get the £30 required to purchase aforementioned footwear and proceed to wear them until the soles wore thin.

Now, as much as I like my Dunlop Green Flash trainers, I liked those too-cute shoes a whole lot more, so Angel and I devised a plan of action.

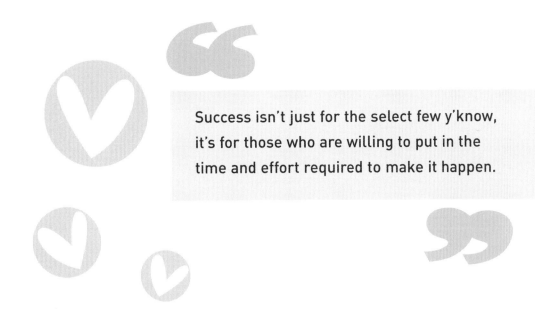

Success isn't just for the select few y'know, it's for those who are willing to put in the time and effort required to make it happen.

We outlined the ultimate goal, which was to own the too-cute pair of shoes and then made a list of all the do-able ways I could earn money. Angel's slightly frazzled next door neighbour Jen was a single mum and we thought she would welcome a break, so I knocked on her door and offered myself as a babysitter. She gratefully accepted. There was a slight flaw in my plan however, because as good as I was with small children, I had never changed a nappy. But after a quick demonstration from Jen, I was not only going to earn money, I could also add nappy-changing to my ever-growing list of things I rock at!

Three Saturday evenings and ten poopy nappies later, I was able to purchase aforementioned gorgeous shoes.

It would have been super easy to make excuses not to babysit, those poopy nappies being one of them, but because I wanted those too-cute shoes so badly I made a commitment to myself to make them mine. I worked hard and I got my reward – they look gorgeous by the way!

Its never too soon to start flexing your action muscles, start by:

☆ Creating good habits - make a to-do list of short-term goals, everything from homework to daily chores - crossing them off feels so good!

☆ Start projects way before they're due. Not only will you get them done on time, you'll probably do a better job coz you're not so rushed.

☆ Stay focused – in the same way that you'll finish your homework sooner without any interruptions, if you stay focused on what it is you want in the world you'll be a huge success!

☆ Make a non-negotiable pact with yourself- when asking yourself to do something that requires effort, it's amazing what wild excuses we can come up with for not getting round to doing them. But remember, these are changes you want to make, goals you want to achieve, if you blow them off the only person that will miss out is you, so make the pact and stick to it like glue.

☆ Once you've achieved, celebrate – after you've achieved a small step towards your goal, be sure to celebrate, rewards will help motivate you and keep you on your destiny driveway!

LIVE LIFE NOW

'...WELL, WHAT YOU WAITING FOR? ...'

For a while my life monumentally sucked.

I had annoying, argumentative parentals, I didn't live in the nicest bit of town, my best friend was at boarding school and - as if that wasn't enough for one girl in the world - I had bad hair, pimples and a chubby tummy. Grrr.

I blamed everyone except myself. Well c'mon, it couldn't possibly be my fault could it?

Except it was.

My negative 'tude was acting like a big super-sized magnet attracting a whole host of badness and sadness to my glitter-less life and the only person able to do anything about it was me.

Your attitude is all yours, chica, if you don't want your life to be full of coulda, woulda, shoulda moments then Think Pink. Flick the switch to positive and fill your life with sunshine and smiles, because the only thing stopping you from being the most amazing, kick-ass version of you is...YOU!

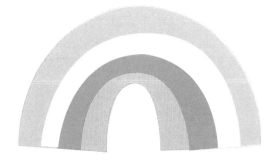

Do you rule your world?

Are you sitting waiting for your life to happen or are you going for gold?

There's a gorgeous fluoro-pink dress in the window of your favourite shop, do you:
a. Love it, but you wouldn't dare wear it, what would people say?
b. Check they've got it in your size and take it straight to the counter.

There are auditions being held for the new school production, do you:
a. Wait to see if anyone you know is signing up.
b. Go to the board and put your name at the top of the list.

You're crushing on a cute dude, do you:
a. Keep crushing, no-one you know has a boyfriend so you'd be the odd one out.
b. Ask him out before someone else snaps him up.

The dude you sit next to in science is slating your mate, do you:
a. Get mad but say nothing.
b. Challenge him about it, that's your mate he's slating!

There's a new arty film on at the cinema, but everyone you ask to go with you is busy, do you:
a. Wait until it comes out on DVD.
b. Buy some popcorn and treat yourself to a date with yourself!

Mostly a's

You are officially 'miss maybe tomorrow', in fact, you'd happily put off living your life if you thought it was actually possible! You worry what people think of you and wait for the green light from others before making decisions – if this continues, you'll miss out on something amazing – your life!

Mostly b's

Hey lil' miss motivated! You can't imagine being anything but yourself and you're always excited about what's around the corner. You're not afraid to speak your mind or to try new things, your life positively rocks!

asking out cute guy at school

Go-for-it Girl...

...Speaks her mind
...Pink cape, natch
...Cute tiara
...Vanity case – utility belts are so Batman and
  Robin

Enter Go for it Girl...Defender of positivity with the power to achieve amazing things!

Method of transformation: pole sliding and spinning in telephone box are not altogether practical and, lets face it, have all been done before so instead I jump up and down on my bed to get any bad stuff out and make room for all the positive sparkly-gorgeous things in my life.

Superhero powers include:
★ Turning a negative situation into a positive
★ Giving things a go
★ Not fearing failure
★ Being confident
★ Taking chances
★ Creating opportunities

Cute optional extras:
★ PMA spray – Positive Mental Attitude in a
  bottle!
★ Glitter gun – the perfect way to bring fun
  and sparkle into your day
★ Lipgloss – to make my lips look pretty,
  duh!
★ A pink positivity magnet – to attract the
  good stuff
★ Go-for-it Girl's mantra: Live life NOW!

Lola the 'Energy Vamp' Slayer

Walking amongst us... are energy vamps...

When my mum found my Project FUTURE dream list pinned to my pink memo board she laughed. As in she laughed out loud. When she finally recovered from her self-induced giggle fit, she said, 'This is all very well, Lola, but what are you really going to do about it?'

I ignored my mother's negative 'tude and proudly announced that I intended to do everything on my list. This caused yet more impromptu laughter from the parental. 'But Lola,' she said, 'you've got to be realistic. These kind of things don't happen to people like us. You should stop daydreaming and start thinking about a real career.'

She was right, we weren't the richest of people, living in the swankiest part of town but this didn't mean I had to limit my dreams just because of my surroundings. No way, in fact it's those things that have made me even more determined to make them happen, every single one of them!

Unfortunately my parental isn't the only person with a negative attitude. Walking amongst us, disguised as humans, are people who don't Think Pink. Although they resemble us on the outside, they are actually energy vamps – set to suck any positive energy and enthusiasm from Pink Thinkers and replace it with the deadliest poison of them all, negative 'tude. Boo.

My mum,
the 'energy vamp'

How to spot an energy vamp:

★ They rarely smile due to the fact they think their life is so monumentally sucky
★ Their vocabulary will consist of words like; 'can't' and 'won't'
★ They will insist on seeing the bad in every situation

Although they are simple to spot, they are not always easy to avoid. They are able to inject their negative 'tude in a matter of minutes, the effects of which, if not dealt with immediately, can be permanent.

The effects:

If affected, it will feel like every negative thought they want you to think about yourself, everything from 'you'll never be able to write a book, you can't even spell' to 'you come from a council estate, you'll never be successful' has been downloaded onto your mini-mp3player. Those thoughts will then become the soundtrack you hear in your head day in day out. If the shuffle button isn't pressed, the negative playlist will become a firm favourite, causing self-esteem levels to drop and self-belief to become non-existent.

How to combat this:

The only way to slay Energy Vamps and their deadly negative 'tude is to Think Pink. Take control by deleting the negative playlist permanently so that you'll never be able to listen to it again and replace it immediately with a whole set of exciting, grrl power type beliefs that will become the new soundtrack to your life.

List all the energy vamps you know (and vow to avoid them from now on!)

....

....

....

....

....

....

....

....

....

....

....

....

....
....
....
....

List all the negative thoughts they downloaded and caused you to think about yourself

....
....
....
....
....
....
....
....
....
....
....
....
....

Now replace each of those negative thoughts with a kick-ass one for your new and improved soundtrack

....
....
....
....
....
....
....
....
....
....
....
....
....
....
....
....

No limits

I wouldn't dream of being seen without my glitter pink lipgloss, so if the lid on my Juicy Tube was stuck shut, I wouldn't give up and go bare-lipped, oh my stars, could you imagine? No, I would simply find another way to make sure my lips looked sparkly-gorgeous. The same applies to your life.

Take Bella for example, she has always dreamed of being lead guitarist in a riot grrl rock band. She went to audition after audition, but no-one wanted her. Did she cuss the

music business? Did she think of giving up? Did she throw monumental hissy fits? Well, yes actually, she did. But right after she did that, she decided to stop following the riff of someone else's bad guitar playing and, instead, start her own band! She enlisted the help of the Pink Ladies: Sadie beats the drums, Angel looks pretty and sings backing vocals and I sing lead vocals and am learning my three chords. The thing is Bella didn't wait for something to happen, she positively made it happen! You've got to create your own opportunities in life.

Fact.

Love to learn

I love leaning, I don't mean maths and stuff, because although essential, it doesn't rate highly on the things that I passionately love and adore, no, I mean the actual act of learning new things. According to the scientific dudes in white coats, learning new things is like exercise for the brain, minus the sweaty, weight lifting bit obviously. It's true. When you try new and different things, not only do you discover new skills, talents and passions but your mind becomes super stimulated providing the added excitement of the limitless possibilities that lie just around the corner!

What would you like to learn?

....
....
....
....
....
....
....
....
....
....
....
....
....
....
....
....
....
....
....
....

You don't always have to take an organised lesson or buy a book to try something new, you'll be surprised at the special talents the people around you have. Whether it's shooting a hoop or painting the perfect picture, ask your friends to pass on a talent, mine have...

Just do it!

Are you ready for your glittery existence to change forever? Because this is the ultimate in Think Pink revelations...

Your life doesn't have to be about what you're going to become in the future, you are feisty, fun, fearless and fabulous and you can do amazing things right now! Start by taking a look at your dream list. Chances are there are things on there that, with a little creative thinking, you'd be able to make happen right now. Check out these things that don't have to wait until I'm a grown up...

Create your own website:
Mine is **www.pink-world.co.uk** and is the online version of the magazine I've always wanted to read! It's got interviews with fashion designers, jewellery makers, artists and writers, features and tips on everything from customising to being successful, it's got cute boys (well it would be rude not to, wouldn't it?) it features real girls who are doing amazing things as well as a whole section dedicated to books – I dig books mostest!

How to make your own site:
1. Search for a freebie Internet Service Provider to host your site.
2. Download a free Web-page editor – like blogger.com – who offer lots of helpful hints on how to build it.
3. Fill your pages with fun – check out www.fg-a.com for ideas on how to enhance your site with pics, wallpaper and buddy icons.
4. Email me with your finished results, I'd love to see them!

Lola@pink-world.co.uk

Learn to Dance...

And I don't just mean bustin' moves around your room (although that's cool too). Organised dance classes are a great way to get to make new friends. They're also a top excuse to buy some way-cool fluro pink Flashdance leg- warmers...

Ballroom dancing might look like it's for the old folks but it's actually really good fun. Sadie's granddad taught us all how to waltz and, oh my stars, it makes me feel just like an old time movie star!

Or how about Street Dancing? It's a really modern style of dancing that's perfect if you're totally into hip hop and want to dance like those dudes on MTV.

For the more adventurous chicas, Salsa dancing is fun and means 'Sauce' in Spanish! It's all about the kickin' and hair flickin' and getting your groove on with a (preferably) hot boy type!

Learn to Cook

Cooking up a storm in the kitchen is all kinds of fun. It means I don't have to rely on anyone else to provide me with a hot tray of freshly baked double double double choc chip cookies when I need them! It also means that when I leave home, I'll be super independent and not have to live on pizzas forever.

This is one of my fave recipes and it's really easy to make it for all your Pink Ladies.

Pasta Pesto x 4
You will need:
☆ Eight handfuls of pasta
☆ One tablespoon of olive oil
☆ One jar of green pesto
☆ 50g of grated cheese

How to make it:
☆ Boil the pasta according to the pack instructions. I like my pasta a bit crunchy.

☆ Once the pasta is cooked, drain it (be careful not to splash that boiling water on your sparkly self!) and pour it back into the empty pan.

☆ Add two big tablespoons of pesto to the pasta and mix it through so all the pasta is covered.

☆ Now add the olive oil to make your pasta even yummier.

☆ Before you serve to the Pink Ladies, sprinkle over some grated cheese.

☆ Now you're a domestic goddess, you can add all sorts of delish things to the basic pasta pesto like roast chicken, mushrooms, red peppers, tuna - the list is endless!

Remember to ask the parentals to help with the oven if it's your first time and don't forget to do the washing up!

Write a book

You can write a book from the moment you can pick up a pen or tap a computer, so what are you waiting for? Cathy Cassidy, the incredibly successful author of Dizzy and Indigo Blue offers would-be writers this advice:

✩ Don't listen to the people who say you can't do it – if you want to do something badly enough, you can.

✩ Live life to the full – have adventures, have fun, be happy, be sad. Write about what you care about, what moves you – put your feelings into your work.

✩ Read like crazy and write – every day, if possible. These are the best ways to learn your trade. Hopefully, one day other people will be reading your work!

For more advice and tips check out: **www.cathycassidy.com**

Learn to...write Haiku

Sadie is poetic, she writes odes to guitar boys and songs that will make your heart ache, she also writes Haiku...

I discovered Haiku when I visited Japan with my mucho older bro, who was working there as an English teacher (lucky boy and official male Think Pinker!). It's one of the most traditional forms of Japanese poetry and is so much fun. Basically Haiku means 'short verse' which is exactly what it is. It's got 17 syllables – five in the first line, seven in the second and five in the last. They can be about anything. Some of the best I've read describe daily situations in a brand new way. Try it!

I HEAR THE GUITAR
I'M LOST IN THE MAGIC SOUND
AND MY HEART BEATS FAST

NICE BOYS CAN'T PLAY ROCK
THEY ARE WAY TOO SWEET FOR THAT
STICK TO POP INSTEAD

I WILL NOT GET BACK
THE FIFTEEN MINUTES I CRUSHED
ON SIMON COWELL

Learn to...play the guitar

Bella is a guitar playin' goddess, she taught me to play C, A and D chords in one evening by writing numbers on my left hand...

So you wanna be a guitar girl?

Number your fingers on your left hand with a felt tip then, starting with chord C, it's the easiest, match it up with the beautifully drawn chart. The lines going across are strings, the lines going down are frets, put your fingers in position and with your right hand, strum!

Practise, practise, practise each one, then when you feel comfy, start playing them faster and together until you can switch between different chords without having to think about it...You're officially a guitar girl – woohoo!

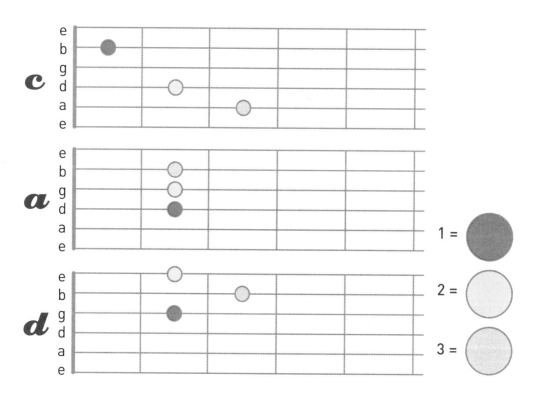

Learn to...apply lipstick

Angel prides herself on the fact she can apply a full face of make-up without a mirror, it's not her only talent, but it is the one she is currently most proud of...

Applying lipstick so that it doesn't come off mid-smooch is an art form sweetie, but follow these five easy steps and you'll be able to pout with pride before and after...

1. Brush your lips lightly with a toothbrush to remove any yucky dried skin
2. Define your lips by using a lip liner that matches your lipstick
3. Apply lipstick using a brush
4. Blot your lips by placing a piece of tissue between your lips and dust over tissue with face powder, this fixes it in place
5. Repeat the whole process from number 2 and finish by putting a little lip gloss in the centre of your bottom lip – voila! The perfect pout!

Going for Gold

Take a look at anyone who has achieved success in some area of their life, and you will see that the main reason for that success was an unshakeable belief in their idea or ability to succeed. It really is that simple.

★ Be your own cheerleader – enlisting a troupe of over-enthusiastic pom pom girls to support and motivate you on a daily basis just isn't practical, so make sure you say positive, butt-kicking things to yourself every day. Try these:

'you're the best'

'you're super creative'

'you can do it'

★ Take risks – it pays to take chances, because the only wrong decision you could make would be not to make one at all.

★ Face your fears – whether that's a person or a task you've been dreading – dare ya!

★ Don't sweat if you fail – so your lad's dumped you, you didn't get picked for a team, you failed a test…It's not a failure, it's experience, learn from it and move on!

★ Be persistent – it might not happen first time round, but if you want it enough, it will happen.

★ Take control – only you can get the things you want in life, so haul yourself off the sofa and make it happen!

Write your own fairytale

Forget the days when fairytales were all about girls waiting for Prince Charming to provide the perfect happy ending, every Think Pink princess knows that the most bliss-kissed life is only achievable when you face up to a challenge and never give up!

It's easy to want to stay under the duvet and avoid anything that makes us fearful but just think of all the amazing, fun, sunshine-filled moments that we would miss out on? How your story develops is up to you chica, you're the author of your book, the star of your show, so take charge and give yourself something to smile about...

Think Pink = a feisty, fun, fearless and fabulous YOU!

* ☆ You're beautiful – inside and out.
* ☆ You dream big, exciting dreams.
* ☆ You can wear scuffed trainers, jeans and a tee-shirt and treat them like a ball gown.
* ☆ You see beauty and glitter-filled potential in everything.
* ☆ You're YOU-nique – and that's such a good thing!

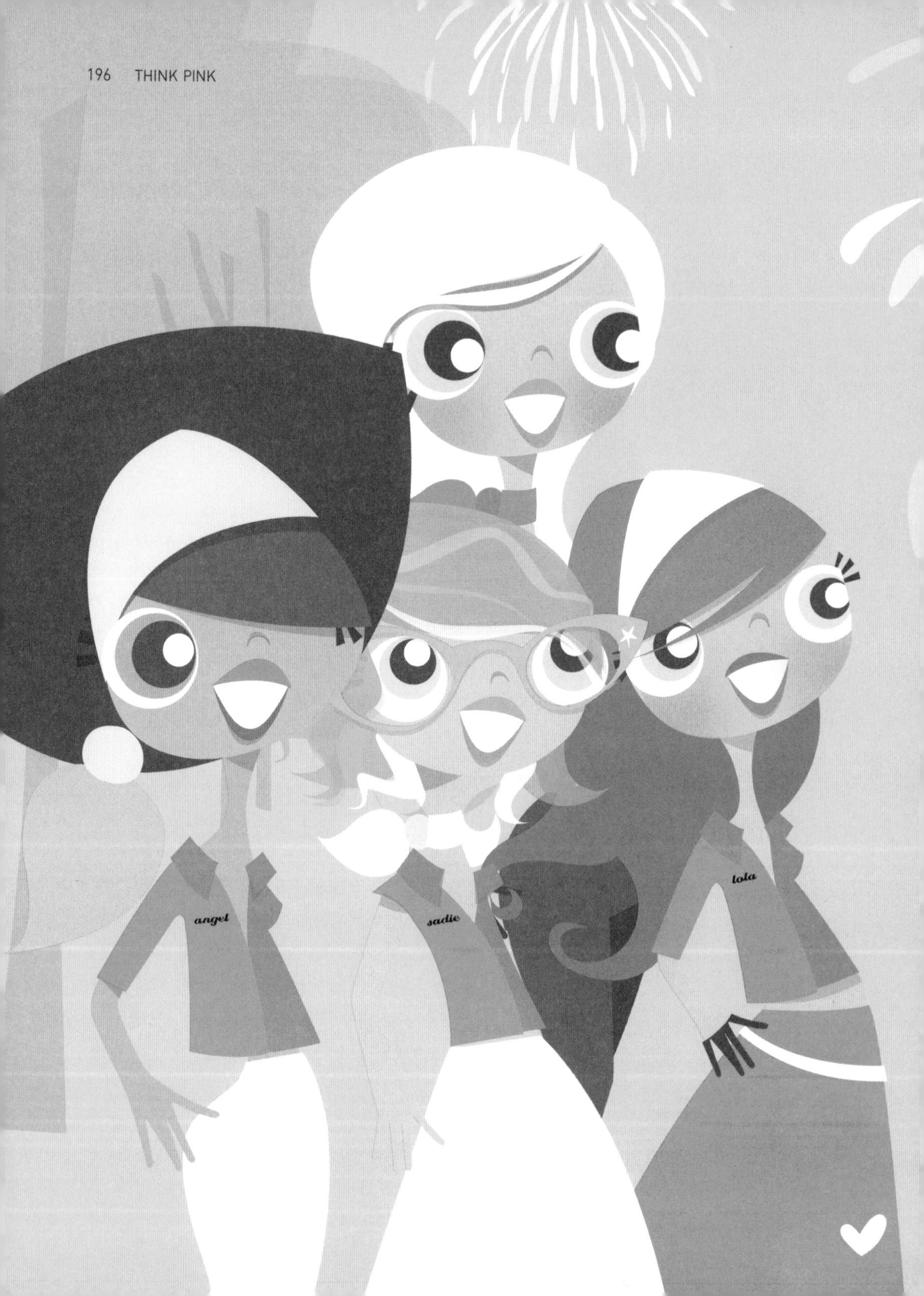
angel
sadie
lola

Until next time,
lots of love and star-shine sparkles....

Lola
xx

I hereby swear to
always think pink

signature.............................

date.............................

Lola

Sadie